Foundations
of the Path

CLIMB THE HIGHEST MOUNTAIN SERIES

Foundations of the *Path*

Mark L. Prophet·Elizabeth Clare Prophet

SUMMIT UNIVERSITY  PRESS®

Corwin Springs, Montana

FOUNDATIONS OF THE PATH
by Mark L. Prophet and Elizabeth Clare Prophet.
Copyright © 1999 by Summit University Press.
All rights reserved.

Library of Congress Catalog Card Number: 99-63313
ISBN: 0-922729-53-0

SUMMIT UNIVERSITY � PRESS®

Summit University Press and 🌺 are registered trademarks.
Printed in the United States of America

Cover: *Remember,* a painting by Nicholas Roerich

04 03 02 01 00 99   6 5 4 3 2 1

I dedicate this book to
El Morya, Kuthumi and Djwal Kul,
whose vision is leading this civilization to its summit.
May we follow them every step of the way
until the earth and its people
are victorious in the light and free.

Contents

2 · Ascended and Unascended Masters   53

3 · The Summit Lighthouse 75

4 · The Messengers 95

7 · The One Path above the Many: Mysticism   217

Notes   229

Glossary   241

Figures

Editor's Preface

THE CLIMB THE HIGHEST MOUNTAIN series represents a unique opportunity to study the mysteries of the ages through the perspective of the Ascended Masters. These books contain the understanding they have gained through millennia of grappling with the human condition on earth. Applying their collective wisdom to your life can help you do what they have done—unite wholly, immortally with God. To immerse yourself in the spiritual currents these pages carry is to receive a direct transfusion of their light.

The Ascended Masters are the saints and sages of East and West who have graduated from earth's schoolroom and become one with God. They are in contact with the hearts, minds and souls of all of earth's people. They teach and guide each one who is open to their ministrations. Many of their students do not outwardly know that they are cherished disciples of one or more of our immortal brothers and sisters. But as we read the Masters' teachings, many of us recognize them instantly. The teachings have a familiar ring that can key us into inner experiences woven through both our waking life and our times of rest, when we study with the Ascended Masters at spiritual levels while our body and outer mind sleep.

In the 1960s, the Ascended Masters commissioned the Climb the Highest Mountain series as the "Everlasting Gospel" of the Aquarian age. The style is purposely didactic and often compressed, for it embodies a universality intended to be applicable to all cultures that will appear on earth during the next two thousand years. It is left to the reader to apply the teachings to his own time and circumstance.

The first book in this series was published in 1972 as *Climb the Highest Mountain: The Path of the Higher Self.* The current volume is the second in the series, and the remaining three books are being prepared for publication.

Throughout this work, the authors draw upon and quote from the teachings of the Ascended Masters. This treasure-house of wisdom is as timeless and universally applicable as other presentations of Truth released by the Masters through the ages. These include such living spiritual classics as Helena Blavatsky's *Secret Doctrine,* the Bhagavad Gita, the Tao Te Ching, the many sutras of the Buddha Gautama, the Bible, *The Imitation of Christ* by Thomas à Kempis and the Tibetan Book of the Dead. Thus the Climb the Highest Mountain series is offered as progressive revelation, a priceless addition to the ageless body of scripture, wisdom teachings and inspirational works available to spiritual aspirants.

While working on these volumes with Mrs. Prophet, I have been moved and gratified at the depth of wisdom and loving understanding of the divine and human conditions they contain. Day by day, I could feel a joy bubbling within her in anticipation of the treasury of spiritual keys about to be given to spiritual seekers throughout the world.

Some of the teachings in this volume are condensed seed concepts that await your meditation to unfold them. To enhance this process the following books are recommended for further study. *The Chela and the Path* by the Ascended Master El Morya and *Cosmic Consciousness* by Mark L. Prophet provide a basic grounding in Ascended Master concepts. For an explanation of the Cosmic Clock, which this volume refers to liberally, see *The Great White Brotherhood in the Culture, History and Religion of America* by Elizabeth Clare Prophet.

The Science of the Spoken Word by Mark L. Prophet and Elizabeth Clare Prophet and *The Creative Power of Sound* by Elizabeth Clare Prophet introduce the practice of decreeing, which is used to draw God's light into action on earth.

Walking the spiritual path is a joyous though sometimes arduous endeavor. It requires change, especially where parts of one's being have settled into levels of comfortability that stubbornly resist inner growth. Even as Jesus compared developing spiritual power with moving mountains, the Climb the Highest Mountain series conveys the power to change a world —your world.

LLOYD LEIDERMAN

Note: Because gender-neutral language can be cumbersome and at times confusing, we have used the pronouns *he* and *him* to refer to God or to the individual and *man* or *mankind* to refer to people in general. We have used these terms for readability and consistency, and they are not intended to exclude women or the feminine aspect of the Godhead. God is both masculine and feminine. We do, however, use the pronouns *she* and *her* to refer to the soul because each soul, whether housed in a male or a female body, is the feminine counterpart of the masculine Spirit.

Introduction

One of the mighty angels John the Revelator encountered gave him a little book. The angel commanded him to "take it, and eat it up; and it shall make thy belly bitter, but it shall be in thy mouth sweet as honey."[1] The volume you hold in your hand is such a book.

It is a discourse on Cosmic Law set down in words that will bring to you the sweetness of divine illumination as you "eat it up." For in your exposure to the Law is found a sense of great joy and great sweetness of God consciousness. But when you begin to digest the Law, a chemicalization begins wherein darkness becomes light.

The light's encounter with the darkness of past karma is like the contact of two incompatible chemicals that produces an explosion. Darkness cannot contain light, and therefore it is transformed. It is like turning a light switch on or off in a closed room. There is either light or darkness, but they don't occupy the same space.

During the years that I [Elizabeth] worked with Mark on the volumes of the Climb the Highest Mountain series, I would sit in my meditation room at La Tourelle in Colorado Springs and Messengers of God would come to bring scrolls of concepts that showed how they wanted them outlined in various chapters. The revelations were given, and they were so high that sometimes I would groan because of the influx of the concept and the consciousness of the Masters upon my consciousness. On many occasions, I had to say to the Messenger of God, "This is all I can take for today. I can't take any more." And I experienced this bitterness in the belly, the chemicalization of Truth in my consciousness.

My state of attunement had to be very, very high to be able to stand in the presence of Cosmic Beings delivering their outlines for this series, which is intended to be scripture for the new age. It was like the experience of John on the Isle of Patmos, when the angel of Jesus came to him and he was transported to a very high state of consciousness. And yet even when John, in this high state of consciousness, took in the concentrated energies of the little book, they exploded. And that bitterness began to transform his whole being.

The purpose of this series is to bring you to the level of attunement at which these revelations were made to me and to Mark. It is not merely to pass on to you intellectual knowledge. You can go up the mountain and sit down and read these books as the Everlasting Gospel, and you'll have the knowledge they contain. But my goal is for your consciousness to be raised so that you will have the same experiences that we had when we received the revelation.

Emerson says to go beyond a book's form to the essence behind it when he asserts: "Talent alone can not make a writer. There must be a man behind the book; a personality... pledged to the doctrines there set forth.... If there be [not] God's word in the man,—what care we how adroit, how fluent, how brilliant he is?"[2] The man behind these books is the hidden man of the heart, the Universal Christ, who will not leave you as he finds you.

The receipt of this series into Mark's and my consciousness demanded total sacrifice, total selflessness, total surrender of our personal lives, a laying down of our lives for the Masters. And we are dedicated to continuing this service in your behalf. We want you to know that as you read the Climb the Highest Mountain series, you can call to God and our Higher Self for understanding, for the integration of the light into your being. We will be with you at inner levels. We will use the authority of our office to assist you in your spiritual quest.

The wise reader will understand that the Path is both simple and complex. The simple truths of life ingrained in every heart and mind are keys to a vast compendium of knowledge that the LORD has hidden from the worldly-wise and made known to the pure in heart. Thus continual study and a guileless application to one's Higher Self (the Christ within) are prerequisites to assimilating life's sweetest and most sacred mysteries.

These are the mysteries of the Ancient of Days, who has promised to write his laws in our inward parts so that all might know him, from the least unto the greatest.[3] And this he has done. Even so, many find it difficult to clearly understand the Law of their being. Its subtleties are inscrutable, because the Law is written in a language that is inaccessible to those who will read only outer signs and symbols where an inner sense (a holy innocence) is required.

But what, then, of those who are caught between the dark and the daylight? What of those who would touch the hem of the Master's garment and enter into the kingdom, yet they cannot because they see not? These need signposts along the way to guide them until they can hear the sound of his voice and the rustle of his robes.

As Messengers of the Great White Brotherhood, Mark

and I have dedicated ourselves to creating those signposts, and many are included in this series. These teachings are calculated to lead seekers into the Promised Land of their own God-free being. Through this knowledge and the assistance of the Ascended Masters that accompanies the worded expression, the reader is offered a grander vision and a lifeline of hope in an age of crisis.

The Truth we present in this work is given in the tradition of progressive revelation. As one by one, students go unto their Father (the Presence of God within), greater revelations will be added unto them. It is our great desire that the keys in these volumes lay the foundation for a golden age that will come because the students of Ascended Master Law incorporate these keys into their lives.

When mankind en masse learn the higher way of living, of praying, and of invoking light—practicing the sacred science—they will resurrect the cultures of civilizations that existed 300,000 to 500,000 years ago. And they will discover the secrets of health, longevity, alchemical precipitation—the mastery of the physical universe. But most important, they will also have dominion in spiritual realms and learn the way of the immortals.

The Truth we set forth herein is the Truth of the ages, the laws whereby the universes were framed. This is the Truth that is locked in the memory of the atoms and cells that compose the earth's crust and the being of man. This is the Truth that every soul knows. But without proper training and education it has remained lost, lying dormant just beneath the surface of the mind until it is brought to the fore by contact with the light and renewed by the Teachers, the Ascended Masters, who stand waiting in the wings, ready to disclose the missing pieces to the puzzle of life.

All that man requires to complete his evolution and fulfill his divine plan will be revealed to him through the indwelling

Christ, the indwelling Buddha and the memory of the soul awakened, quickened and mobilized by the heavenly hosts. Nothing will be withheld from those who diligently pursue the knowledge of the Law of life. Man's fulfillment lies in the desire to be more of God, more of his higher consciousness, more of life.

As Naaman the Syrian was required to dip into the river Jordan seven times to be healed of his leprosy,[4] so we ask that those desiring a transformation of consciousness immerse themselves in the light of the Seven Spirits of God that permeates these pages that they might receive their momentum of God-awareness, the momentum of Elohim.

In so doing, realize that reading this book (like all experience in the planes of Matter) is a means to an end, not an end in itself. The goal is God consciousness, which is always in turn a means to another end: greater God consciousness. For God is always growing, and you are a catalyst that fosters that growth even while your God Presence fructifies unfolding grace on earth.

As you read, we would have you hear the whispers of the universe in heart and mind, brood with the Great Spirit over the rites of creation, cast yourself in the cosmic drama reenacting the ritual of a cosmos, a rose, a cell, an idea. Involve yourself in reality and thereby secure the mastery of self, of destiny.

As Messengers for the spiritual hierarchy, we have been commissioned to speak the unspeakable, to utter the unutterable, and to set forth in writing what no man has written. Ours is to make plain in earthly tongue what heretofore has been penned in the tongues of angels, to make clear the precepts of love.

Newfound freedom will come not alone from the formed but from the unformed, not only from what is said but from what remains unsaid. For words are but cups into which the mind and heart must pour the substance of experience and devotion, the distillations of soul knowing, the formulations that are idling just beneath the surface of awareness—waiting for the radiant peace of the Buddha and the power of the Christ to bring them to light.

The spinning wheel of life conspires so marvelously to produce the garment of your soul, so gossamer and filmy—raiment that will one day become a garment of solar radiance, of attainment. It weaves the wedding garment that you will wear as living devotion and love's perfect shield against delusion, confusion and misunderstanding.

Enfolded in this mantle of light, may you open the door of your heart to a renewal of your life in the alchemical furnace of the inner man, who loves you most. And may the angels from the realms of glory sit on your shoulder as you pursue these words and ever guide you into the Truth you seek.

In service to God in you,

Mark L. Prophet

Elizabeth Clare Prophet

MARK AND ELIZABETH PROPHET
Messengers for the Great White Brotherhood

Chapter 1

The Great White Brotherhood

The White Brotherhood . . . is a stronghold of knowledge, and a treasury of life-giving energy. Verily, the whole world and its humanity are held together only by these Guardians!

HELENA ROERICH

The Great White Brotherhood

THE GODDESS OF LIBERTY would draw all men into the cooperative spirit of universal liberty under the banner of the Great White Brotherhood.* For through such a union will the souls of earth achieve their divinely appointed destiny. She explains: "The thrust of man's desire for liberty has its origin in the very sun center of the universe. Man was conceived in the expansive flame of liberty from God's own heart. This reality, dimmed now by intruding factors, remains the goal of the wise and the sincere.

"The billions who call the planet earth home are broken fragments of a universal oneness. The liberty of oneness has been lost to the multifaceted sense of separation, and thus beneath his own fig tree and attached to his own vine,[1] man goes his separate and several ways.

---

*The Great White Brotherhood is a spiritual order of hierarchy, an organization of Ascended Masters united for the highest purposes of God in man as set forth by Jesus Christ, Gautama Buddha and other world teachers. The word "white" refers not to race, but to the white light of the Christ that surrounds the saints and sages of all ages who have risen from every nation to be counted among the immortals.

"No specific good would occur in the community of being by forcing the separated segments of the Universal into an unwilling alliance. For there the liberty of oneness would be ignored and the pull of the senses, like snorting wild steeds, would create its tides of restless energy to pull man away from the balance of true being.

"Only the pull of the sun center of universal reality, only the recognition by mankind en masse of the great laws governing cosmos and the spread of understanding about cosmos can develop within the unfolding identity of the individual a sense of the harmony of universal liberty."[2]

Renewed Opportunity

Trailing clouds of glory, the children of Alpha and Omega come into the world fresh from the octaves of light, vowing to do God's will and to fulfill the noble plan. Descending in a spiral of light, consciousness involutes, rolling into a ball of fire as it draws within itself the light-potential for another round of evolution.

The soul, which had full awareness at the end of the previous cycle, in the twinkling of an eye becomes once again an embryonic god. Spiraling into the birth canal, it loses the memory of former lives and friendships, of buoyant life at inner levels. The veil of mercy falls, but the positive and negative momentums of the soul's past development remain as a sheath of identity.

Secured within the heart is the seed containing the nourishment of solar (soul) destiny. The keys for every right decision are locked within the etheric body. The voice of conscience becomes the steady compass that will guide the frail bark across the high seas of adventure in the world of form.

Through a tunnel of innocence the soul comes, only to find civilization with all its accoutrements waiting like a mammoth beast, eager to devour her purity. The distant memory of exalted spheres makes the soul unwary. How dense the world has become! She is slow to learn its ways.

The Thirst for Brotherhood

The world to which the soul has come is far from being a reflection of the etheric cities and temples of light where she has sojourned between embodiments. As her fiery ball of consciousness continues to penetrate lower and lower levels, the soul eventually reaches her farthest point of descent. There the dilemma of the ages becomes an unbearable weight. Suddenly she realizes that she is caught between the synthetic world and the real world, not really a part of either one. Vows easily taken at airy heights become a cross.

An idealist in her youth, the soul would turn society inside out and level injustice with a clenched fist and a loud outcry: "It's all wrong!" But those who have become accustomed to the darkness of unreality do not understand her plea.

The soul knows that there are rules to the game of life, formulas that unlock the secrets of overcoming, laws that govern the release of energy. These keys to reality provide the links in the chain of being, and without them neither child nor childman can make substantial inroads into the existing structures and established traditions that have perpetuated evil as well as good through the centuries.

Entering into the mainstream of life, the soul is often caught in the undercurrents of mass movements and vortices of hatred, prejudice, war and the manipulations of the Luciferians (those who followed Lucifer in his rebellion against God). She cries out for help, and her elder brothers and sisters, who have charted the course before her, heave her the lifeline of the Great White Brotherhood.

The Great White Brotherhood's Reason for Being

The Great White Brotherhood's primary function is to return mankind's consciousness to the liberty of oneness by disseminating an understanding of cosmos—the unerring Law that governs the cycles and destiny of the microcosm (man) and the Macrocosm (his true home of light).

In this chapter we unveil the Brotherhood that you might make direct contact with your elder brothers and sisters, who are fully qualified to lead you out of the synthetic environment of earth.

The Creator in his wisdom knew from the beginning the consequences of man's misuse of the gift of free will. He foresaw each wrong decision as a negative spiral drawing man downward into shadowed resentment and the darkness of self-delusion—begetting fear, doubt, rebellion and finally total separation from the creative plan and from the freedom of good will.

Having seen how the darts of pride had penetrated the earth and planets in other systems of worlds, God knew that it would take only a few rebellious lifestreams to puncture the balloons of personal happiness for millions of his children. God therefore prepared a way whereby eternal Truth might be preserved in every system of worlds, on every planetary body where the children of the sun were sent with wings on their heels to evolve the plan of life.

Inasmuch as all humanity came forth from God and were intended to fulfill his plan, the Father (knowing the end from the beginning) conceived of a great brotherhood of light, an eternal brotherhood wherein those of more advanced attainment on the Path would help their brothers and sisters of lesser attainment.

God intended cooperation among his children—a blending of the light rays, a weaving of the threads of light that form the universal deathless solar body (the antahkarana, the web of life), each thread maintaining its identity while at the same time contributing to the universal oneness.

Mary Baker Eddy, founder of Christian Science, glimpsed this cosmic conception of the brotherhood of man under the Fatherhood of God when she wrote in *Science and Health with Key to the Scriptures:* "God gives the lesser idea of Himself for a link to the greater, and in return, the higher always protects the lower. The rich in spirit help the poor in one grand brotherhood, all having the same Principle, or Father; and blessed is that man who seeth his brother's need and supplieth it, seeking his own in another's good."

Glimpsing the grand fraternity of light-beings, she remarked: "The universe of Spirit is peopled with spiritual beings, and its government is divine Science.... Advancing spiritual steps in the teeming universe of Mind lead on to spiritual spheres and exalted beings." And observing the service of the Builders of Form, she said, "The eternal Elohim includes the forever universe."[3]

The Formation of the Great White Brotherhood

The idea of the Brotherhood was born in the Mind of God through the universal Christ consciousness who is the Logos, the pure light of the Great White Way. God the Father could neither behold evil nor look upon iniquity, but through the Christ he was in touch with every situation in the universe. The Christ intelligence endowed the Father's concept for his creation with the tangible reality of the Great White Brotherhood. Thus was born the seamless garment of the universal Christ consciousness.

The Brotherhood is the hope of every man. It is God's plan for the orderly expression of his love. It is his provision for raising the individual by raising the whole, as well as for raising the whole through individual attainment. The Brotherhood is an effective means whereby God reaches out secretly to perform his wonders of deliverance and his miracles of salvation to a world that has departed the path of righteousness.

Although spiritual in origin, the Great White Brotherhood maintains a very real contact with people on the earth today. Higher initiates are aware of their contact with the Brotherhood, whereas lesser aspirants work and serve without any conscious knowledge of their tie. The Great White Brotherhood also functions on other planets and in other systems of worlds.

Agents of the Brotherhood on Earth

At one time the Brotherhood adopted a resolution under the aegis of the Karmic Board whereby some of the hidden mysteries and hidden power of past ages would be released into the hands and use of some advanced chelas (disciples) of the Masters who had demonstrated balance and responsibility over a long period of their lives.[4]

These individuals were given the power and authority to act as a point of contact with the Brotherhood in the world of form to establish certain talismans upon the planet. These talismans would counteract the compelling negatively qualified forces that have enslaved the minds of both the youth and aged alike. Absolute humility was necessary in those to whom these powers were given.

Although the Brothers in White made no physical contact with these initiates, each one was given a mystical experience activating internal spiritual powers together with the understanding of how to use these powers. An index of action and a plan of cooperation with the invisible Brotherhood was also released with that dispensation.

Mighty focuses of light would be anchored in the world of

form enabling mankind to break the power of untoward habit, including the use of intoxicants and narcotics, the wrong use of knowledge or of tongue, propensities for ego-strutting, or the vanity of wasted energy.

The Maha Chohan, representative of the Holy Spirit, explained: "New clarity coming into the mind will enable many among the students to have a greater measure of attunement with their own God Presence, I AM. A sense of personal well-being under God and of universal brotherhood will permeate the atmosphere of the planet. It will make many among mankind more vitally aware of the Holy Spirit in its active participation in human affairs. This will be a means of deliverance for the earth from the perils of past ages and decades—a release from the intensification of mortal delusion and a clarification of the earth's place in the solar scheme."[5]

Cosmic Service

The members of this spiritual fraternity represent the Godhead as rays of light flooding forth from the sun, each one carrying an aspect of the Creator's consciousness and making it practical to embodied souls. One of the best-known members of the Brotherhood is the Ascended Master Jesus Christ, whose Galilean ministry was a magnificent fulfillment of centuries of intense preparation and millennia of divine intent.

The higher initiates of the Brotherhood are known as "the Lords of the Flame," for it is recorded in the Bible that "our God is a consuming fire." "The angel of the LORD appeared unto [Moses] in a flame of fire out of the midst of a bush: and he looked, and, behold, the bush burned with fire, and the bush was not consumed." Out of the midst of the bush God said unto him, "I AM THAT I AM."[6] By this we know that God is a flame who has individualized himself in the flaming identity of his many servant sons.

The Representatives of God Come to Earth

The first representatives of hierarchy on earth were the seven beloved Archangels, who focused the power of the seven rays and nourished the consciousness of the first root race with the love, wisdom and power of the Universal Christ.

With them came the beloved Manu (the progenitor of the root race) and his twin flame—fresh from the universal Causal Body—representing the Father-Mother God to the children of the sun. The Manu represented the Ascended Master consciousness to which all aspired and which all were destined to attain. For in their sojourns in each of the twelve spheres of the Causal Body, the Manu and his twin flame had studied and gained not only mastery over self but also mastery over the four elements under the twelve hierarchies of the sun.

As Gautama Buddha says, "The universe is a cosmic playpen in which God sits with eyes of wonder, awaiting the moment when humanity will finally recognize who they are. And as they do, they will speak God's name, I AM, and the child will be a man."⁷ So the lifestreams of the first root race came forth to their playpen earth as gods in embryo—rejoicing, expanding and serving together.

The Essence of Brotherhood

A root race is a design from the heart of God, a solar mandala. Each point of the geometric form, intricate as embroidered lace, is represented by a son-daughter of God—twin flames destined to outpicture a facet of the design through the monadic whole, the androgynous sphere that was their origin.

Representing the seven rays in perfect balance, as well as the 144 virtues of the Godhead, a root race is a unit of hierarchy, complete in itself for the purpose it is destined to fulfill.

It is endowed with the native affections of brotherhood, which come from the illumined consciousness that sees that each Monad occupies the central position for twelve other Monads.

The cellular structure of brotherhood is like a DNA chain, each link carrying his flame, doing his part, sharing the beauties of God reflected in his energy pool, enhancing the mission of every other Monad.

Thus, brotherhood creates a chain reaction of joy—waves of light rippling through the interconnecting antahkarana of souls wedded to a common purpose and fulfilling that purpose by the geometric law.

Wherever souls are evolving toward oneness, there is brotherhood in action—an instinctive rapport of heart-flames intertwined, braiding energies in a common bond and a common strength, dancing around the maypole of the white fire core.

Without brotherhood, this golden chain mail of strength born of union cannot be forged. Without brotherhood, sunbeams do not merge. Without brotherhood, there is no contact between souls; hence the cosmic flow is absent. Without brotherhood, love is unexpressed; and without brotherhood, structures that would carry the triune energies of Father, Son and Holy Spirit disintegrate.

Manus: Sponsors of the Root Races

When all was in readiness and the descent of the first root race was imminent, the Manu and his twin flame superimposed the pattern of their hierarchical design within and around the planetary body. This pattern is the antahkarana, or web of hierarchy, consisting of the twelve points on the Cosmic Clock (each one connecting with the others) and the point in the center connecting with each of the twelve on the periphery. This mandala, shown in figure 1, represents a matrix for the unfoldment of the thousand-petaled lotus at the crown chakra.

Before God can appoint them to the hierarchical office of Manu, twin flames must outpicture within their own forcefield and consciousness the full mastery of this hierarchical pattern. They must become the diadem in full expression. The masculine Manu focuses his consciousness in the center of the pattern, whereas the representative of the feminine ray focuses the consciousness of the Motherhood of God on the periphery.

Within this replica of the diamond-shining Mind of God we see the interaction of the Alpha-to-Omega, the single atom,

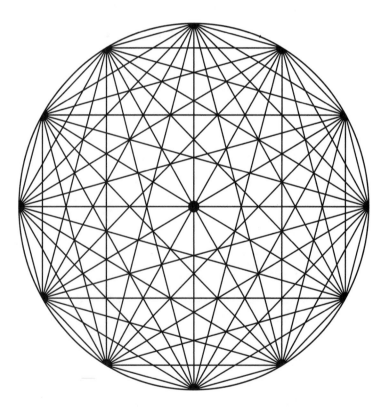

FIGURE 1: The mandala of the Manus and their twin flames.
Focus of their hierarchical design.

comprising the totality of the Father-Mother God in manifestation—which each set of twin flames is one day destined to become. Each intersection of the lines on the pattern is a focal point for initiation, for a release of cosmic energy and for a position in hierarchy. All of the services of the Great White Brotherhood come forth from this hierarchical plan.

The Ritual of Descent

The lowering of the design from the consciousness of the Manu to the planet is a magnificent ritual. The Seven Archangels take their positions within the pattern that is held within the Manu's consciousness. Standing in a circle and facing the center point, they are at that moment actually a part of the thousand-petaled lotus of the Manu himself.

If this is hard to understand, let us think of the question that is often used to relate time and space to infinity: "How many angels can stand on the head of a pin?" Now we ask, "How many Archangels can stand on the head of a Manu?" The answer in both cases is "An infinite number," because there is no limitation of time or space in the Ascended Masters' consciousness. Therefore, existing within the hierarchical pattern is opportunity for an infinite expansion of service, initiation and the expansion of the light through the representatives of hierarchy.

Figure 2 shows eleven points on the circumference of the circle between each pair of the twelve major lines of the Cosmic Clock, which always represent the twelve hierarchies of the sun. These points being equidistant from one another form the same pattern as the major lines of the Clock in groups of twelve, and each pattern represents a progressive turn of the gear in the wheel of the diamond-shining Mind of God.

As subsequent root races embody upon a planet, each one building upon the momentum of the service of the previous

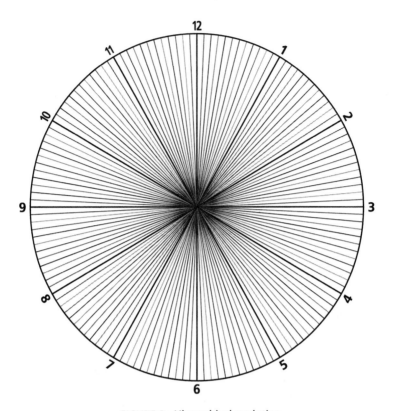

FIGURE 2: Hierarchical evolution.
The pattern of the twelve hierarchies of the sun is progressively rotated
according to the law of cycles, as the root races evolve on earth.

root race, we find that the pattern of hierarchy becomes
increasingly intricate and the Spirit of the Great White Brotherhood becomes more powerful.

During this magnificent ritual wherein the pattern in the
mind of the Manu is transferred to the planetary orb, each of
the Archangels forms a circle around the focal point of consciousness that is the Manu. In figure 3 we see the seven inter-
sections that occur on each of the twelve lines coming from the
center to the periphery of the mandala. These indicate the focal
points of the seven rays, which are directed through the

consciousness of the Seven Archangels.

In figure 4 the bands of the five secret rays are depicted between the white and the yellow bands. The secret rays actually interpenetrate the seven spheres and the focal points of the seven rays in all twelve hierarchies of the sun. The secret rays are discussed further in chapter 6 (see pages 160–67).

As Above, so below. The plan is the same for the ascended Brotherhood as it is for the members of the root race who are

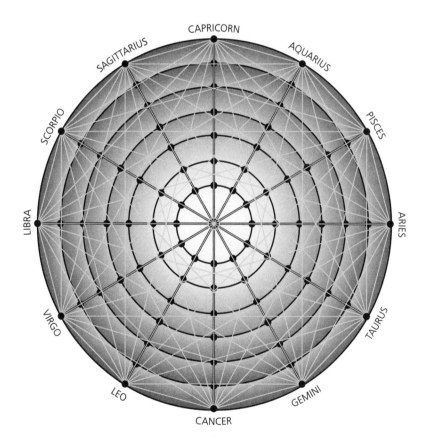

FIGURE 3: Transferring the pattern of the Manu to the planetary orb.
The Seven Archangels assume positions within the pattern at seven points corresponding to the seven rays for each hierarchy of the sun.

to outpicture the plan of brotherhood when they embody. The Manu therefore holds the central position between heaven and earth. He is the connecting point between the kingdom of this world and the kingdom of our God. He holds the pattern of the City Foursquare (the cosmic cube) in behalf of the evolutions who are to embody.

At the precise cosmic moment, the transfer is made and the Archangels take their positions around the planetary body. It is their responsibility, together with the Manu, to teach the

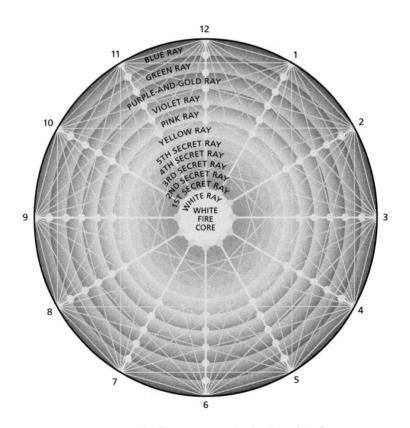

FIGURE 4: The five secret rays in the Causal Body.
The five secret rays interpenetrate the hierarchical design of the Manu,
the order of the seven spheres of the Archangels and the focal points
of the seven rays. See also figure 5, page 161.

incoming lifestreams how to prepare for and pass the initiations that are required before they may take their positions in the Great White Brotherhood in fulfillment of the divine plan for the root race.

The Seed of Destiny Fulfills God's Plan

The plan of God-government for the earth evolves from this pattern, as does the government of the Great White Brotherhood. Thus, an individual who serves at a certain connecting point on earth will no doubt serve in that same capacity after his ascension as he continues to evolve and to pass greater and greater cosmic initiations in the infinite and orderly cycles of hierarchy.

Once it meshes with the four lower bodies of the earth, the hierarchical pattern becomes a giant magnet. Polarizing with the Great Central Sun Magnet, it draws to the planetary home the lifewave that composes the root race that is to fulfill this unique yet universal plan.

Within each soul destined to fulfill the plan is imparted the seed of the hierarchical design. This includes the pattern of her own individual fulfillment and her own point of relativity within the plan. This is the Law that is written in man's inward parts, the Law of his soul's being and destiny.

At a certain point in his development, each lifestream embraces the pattern of the Divine Will and pours the fires of Divine Love from his heart to regenerate the matrix. He releases a sufficient momentum—a critical mass of energy—through his heart chakra, which enables the full momentum of the plan to illumine the mind.

This outpouring of divine energy crowns his soul with Christ consciousness, the crown of twelve stars that is the key to the unfoldment of the crown chakra. Thus the wisdom of the heart becomes the wisdom of the mind. The product of that union is wisdom in action, the full cosmic power of the divine plan fulfilled through heart, head and hand.

This pattern of the Great White Brotherhood that is emblazoned on every heart is the key to the mainstream of life and light to every soul. It contains the keys to precipitation, to self-mastery, to the cycles of time and eternity, to the development of the Causal Body and the overcoming of the negative spiral that resides in the electronic belt. It also contains the secrets of each individual's cosmic destiny, rebirth, regeneration, transfiguration, resurrection and ascension.

Each individual who meditates on his hieroglyph of light can find the keys to the unfoldment of the seven chakras, each of which has a position within the hieroglyph. And when the individual reaches a certain point of self-mastery, the wholeness of the hieroglyph will be superimposed upon each of his chakras. Through such meditation all can draw upon the power of the Great Central Sun Magnet in the service of the Great White Brotherhood for the salvation of the planet.

The First Three Root Races Ascend

As the members of the first root race completed their individual plan and ascended, they assumed positions in hierarchy, in the creative scheme above, to reinforce their momentums gathered below. Retreats and focuses of the Great White Brotherhood were gradually established, as members of the first root race arose to fill the positions necessary for an ever-expanding and transcendent magnetization of light upon the planetary body.

In the early days of the first root race, the Royal Teton Retreat was opened as the home of the Manu and the focus of the Seven Archangels and their complements, who had also anchored their flames across the planetary body.

The forcefields of the Elohim were likewise intact as the

chakras of the earth, which was then transparent crystal reflecting the seven rays as a replica of the Causal Body. The rays of Alpha and Omega at the North and South Poles held the earth in perfect balance.

The seven root races destined to embody upon this planet come forth in the order of the seven rays. Thus the first root race laid the foundation of the Law, the will of God and the perfect divine plan for all who were to follow thereafter.

After the first root race completed its divine plan and ascended back to the heart of God, the second root race came forth in the same manner as the first, building on the pattern already established. Fulfilling the second ray of divine illumination, they added to the pattern what they had been trained to outpicture in the yellow sphere of the Great Causal Body of God.

The third root race then came forth, completing the threefold flame in Divine Love, and returned to the heart of God.

The perfection of these three golden ages is recorded in akasha upon the planetary body. The full-gathered momentum of these Sons and Daughters of God, all now Cosmic Beings, can be invoked on behalf of the victory of the four remaining root races who are to fulfill their destiny upon this planet. The magnetic forcefield of all that they attained is still anchored within the earth, waiting to be invoked.

The Fly in the Ointment

The interruption of God's plan is well known by students of the esoteric tradition: the fall of the Luciferians, the subsequent coming of the laggards, the degeneration of the fourth root race embodied on Lemuria (Mu) and their failure to ascend —requiring the fifth root race to descend while fallen angels, laggards and members of the fourth root race were still embodied. This coming of the fifth and the sixth root races into an imperfect world contributed to their failure to fulfill their plan.

Once the prideful rebellion of the Luciferians began to influence the high priests of Mu, wedges of darkness were driven into the consciousness of the people, separating them from their Source. Agitation and inharmony broke down the protective sheath of the virgin consciousness that is sustained when people express true brotherhood to one another. Fear and doubt widened the gap between man and man and between man and God.

Once mankind had shown themselves vulnerable to the illusions of duality, the entire planet lost its protection. It was then that solar councils allowed the remnant of laggard souls to embody through the fourth root race.

The Creation of the Great Karmic Board

After the Luciferians came, and then the laggards, the progression of mankind's misqualification of the energies flowing through the seven chakras (beginning with the crown and moving downward) finally reached its lowest point in the fall of Adam and Eve, which involved their misuse of the sacred fire through the base-of-the-spine chakra.

Eve, the mother of all living, symbolizes the principle of motherhood. Adam and Eve took embodiment among the fourth root race on Lemuria. They failed to accept the admonishments of God and were thus driven, as were other members of that race, from the paradise of God's pure consciousness of holy innocence. God himself yet preserves that consciousness, and the Great White Brotherhood sustains it through their flame focuses in retreats throughout the world.

The Great Karmic Board came into being when man was banished from the Garden of Eden. He was made to till the ground out of which he was taken, for the laws of alchemy, of divine precipitation, would no longer operate at the level of duality to which he had descended. The Karmic Board was vested with the authority to mete out divine justice and the return of individual and planetary karma as mankind were able to bear it.

The Brotherhood Works to Raise Man to His Lost Estate

Man became a dual being. He is a spirit, as God is. But he has a soul, born of the flame of the Spirit and possessing a similitude of the Spirit, which he has cast down into the shadowed world of imperfection—the world of good and evil. This was possible because the soul has the potential for both good and evil, but the Spirit always adheres to the immutable laws of God-good.

To regain his lost estate, man must now overcome the evil of which he is aware by a goodness other than his own. The righteousness of God that exalteth a nation must also exalt the individual and restore him to the paradise consciousness from whence he came.

After the fall of the fourth root race, when great darkness was spread abroad upon the earth and there was not enough light to perpetuate the existence of the planet, Sanat Kumara, hierarch of Venus, came to maintain a focus of light at Shamballa to restore the evolutions of earth to their lost estate.

The Great White Brotherhood Serves Man

Shamballa—jewel of the sea, flame of hope for millions without flame and without hope! Shamballa—anchor point of the Great White Brotherhood upon earth! With the coming of Sanat Kumara and the Seven Holy Kumaras and their legions

of light along with other volunteers, the rescue mission of hierarchy as the Great White Brotherhood began on earth.

Mankind's extremity was God's opportunity. The rescue
teams arrived. Their mission: to restore the consciousness of
the children of God to primeval single-eyed vision, to raise
them from the sense of duality, the bottomless pit of carnal
desire into which they had fallen. These lost children, having
cut themselves off from all contact with the Christ, required the
intercession of ascended Sons and Daughters of light. Having
lost the torch, they needed others to keep the flame for them
until they were able.

During the first three golden ages, Ascended Masters,
angelic hosts and elementals walked and talked with those
whose consciousness never departed from the unity of good.
After the Fall, mankind no longer perceived these emissaries of
light. Man's consciousness no longer penetrated the spheres of
purity from which he had fallen.

The Masters retreated from the unholy vibrations of the
world, and their focuses of light became known as "retreats."
Henceforth, only those who qualified would be allowed to
enter these secret places of the Most High God, each one a
focus of the Eden that had been lost—Eden having been the
repository of the divine wisdom to which fallen man no longer
had access.

The representatives of the Great White Brotherhood who
embodied subsequent to the coming of Sanat Kumara held the
vision of their assignment by their common bond of light.
Their plan of action was focalized and held intact through the
mandala of the hierarchical design.

The quantity of light that had been sustained in the focuses
of the Archangels and the Elohim and at the Royal Teton
Retreat had been sufficient for golden-age civilizations. In these
civilizations every lifestream knew himself as the Christ and

drew daily enough energy from the heart of the sun to fulfill his assigned position in the plan.

But the tremendous burden of world karma—the physical weight of misqualified energy that the fallen angels, the laggards and misguided members of the fourth root race superimposed upon the planet—necessitated a much greater release of light to offset the darkness and hold the balance of life on behalf of a planet and a wayward generation.

Later, the conditions present on the planet also corrupted the fifth and sixth root races when they arrived. So the Great White Brotherhood decided not to allow the seventh root race to come to earth until these conditions would be resolved.

Heavenly Specialists

Accordingly, as the energy veil densified and the emissaries of Evil became more highly trained and organized, it became necessary to establish specific branches of service within the Great White Brotherhood for the coordination of the rescue mission. These would make known their findings to all other hierarchical units.

The Great White Brotherhood intensified its activity to develop the Christ consciousness in mankind. The legions of Archangel Michael, always active in their devotion to the will of God, now entered into twenty-four-hour service to protect the emerging Christ consciousness of embodied mankind on all of the seven rays and to report threats to planetary safety.

As more Ascended Servants voluntarily enlisted in the liberation of the evolutions of earth, some joined the focuses of light already established and others opened new retreats of their own. Some of these were on the physical plane, while others remained at the etheric level.

Thus the Ancient of Days and all who followed, increasing

in number up to the present moment, took the vow to keep the flame and to expand the light until every last man, woman and child has found the way home to Paradise Lost. For Sanat Kumara had made the cosmic decision of seeing to it that the earth should not perish.

As it gathers more light through cooperation with unascended mankind, the Great White Brotherhood paves the way for greater dispensations of light to the earth from the heart of the Solar Logoi.

The Great White Brotherhood serves as an integral albeit invisible force within every constructive endeavor in which unascended lifestreams are involved, however small or great. It is dedicated to the implementation of the will of God, the divine plan of the hierarchical blueprint.

Its members strive diligently to lead each child of God to his place in the solar scheme, the crossroads of his destiny, the place where the lines of force merge in the mandala—for at that place is the release of the Christ light within the heart of the atom of self. At that place is the potential for an explosion of the Christ consciousness. Yea, there even a Messiah can be born and through him another complete mandala can be formed.

God-Government

The councils of the Great White Brotherhood consider that their single greatest concern is to establish God-government on earth. For where the governments of the nations reflect Ascended Master Law, the golden rule and the precepts of divine brotherhood, there the individual can evolve the Christ flame and become one with his divinity.

Where governments are unjust, the image of the mandala cannot be outpictured in society. In the days of the first three root races the Manus were the rulers, and those who were appointed to hold office during their reign earned the right to represent the people because they had first represented the light. They had passed their initiations and proved their self-mastery over cosmic forces.

As long as members of the hierarchy were in positions of rulership, the earth prospered. But after the Luciferians fell, many of the high priests on Mu in whom the people had placed their confidence became rebellious and used their powers against one another.

There followed the war of the priests. The images on Easter Island are a reminder of the decadence to which they fell. The invectives they hurled at one another instantly became crystallized in stone. Astral beasts of prey, mass forms and weird images resulted from the coalescing of their hatred. They perverted the Divine Love that had once flowed through their chakras, and it turned to stone.

The Divine Right of Kings

The divine right of kings, which persisted to the eighteenth century, came down to us as tradition from the golden ages when the sons of God were invested with the authority of rulership and fulfilled Plato's ideal of the philosopher-king. But as the dynasties became infiltrated with corrupting elements and the stream was no longer pure, the rulers lost contact with the God Source and they became as other men.

Injustices became so great that the people challenged the divine right of succession. Thus, beginning in the nineteenth century, the Brotherhood endorsed democracy as the means whereby each man would become a king and a priest unto God, developing his Christ potential and being found worthy to rule himself.

With the coming of mass education and the raising of the

consciousness of the people, the Ascended Masters have been able to pave the way for an age of total enlightenment, wherein people would not only understand the Law but would behold the character of the Christ in their elected representatives.

In this way they would return to the system of government endorsed in the beginning, where those who by initiation had earned the right to rule would be elected to office under the guidance of the Christ Selves of the electorate.

Side by side with the plan of the Brotherhood to return mankind to a golden age, the false hierarchy—the forces of darkness—have moved to thwart the Brotherhood's every effort. Through their secret organizations in Europe they undermined Saint Germain's plan for the unification of that continent.

Having failed in his efforts to reestablish liberty in Europe as the Comte de Saint Germain, he came to America and inspired the Constitution upon the early patriots. America came to be the cup of light and freedom to the earth, the virgin wilderness where the World Mother could bring forth the Christ consciousness, building a nation under God that all other nations could emulate.

Just as the Christ showed the way of individual self-mastery, so America was to show the way of national destiny. Only when all nations are brought to the level of the Christ consciousness can union occur.

Government Is Meant to Facilitate God's Plan

Chananda, the head of the Indian Council of the Great White Brotherhood, explains: "Seeing clearly the divine plan, the members of the Brotherhood serve to augment and implement every constructive divine idea reflected in government, the social order, man and nature in order to evolve and exemplify the perfect extension of the kingdom of heaven into tangible material form and the manifestation of God-intended happiness everywhere....

"The perfect God-plan for the whole world must be externalized, but this requires enough highly placed people in the governments of the nations of the world who have vision and legislative know-how....

"Karma, too, plays a part in the affairs of government, but the Lords of Karma have assured the Lord of the World (beloved Gautama) that when the governments of the world are ready and, by reason of the cooperation of their respective leaders, they do accept the divine plan for the earth and its evolutions, a dispensation will then be given that will put the mass karma of the entire earth under a special form of cosmic control.

"Under this system all lifestreams will be able to enter some form of temple training at night in their soul bodies and between embodiments. Thus, after passing from physical embodiment, most of the karma that is now outpicturing for them individually can be balanced at inner levels instead of through toil and suffering as is presently the case.

"Mass ascensions will likewise be possible, for a utopian form of world government will automatically eliminate many of the present hazards of living. Struggle for place, position, financial advantage, political power and self-seeking will be replaced by that divine justice which affords—as the Constitution of the United States of America really intends—true equality of opportunity for all.

"In this veritable community of the Spirit where individual dignity is upheld by the light of its own divinity, the communistic and socialistic doctrines will be stripped of their false veneer and revealed to be—as in reality they are—methods that were evolved humanly as the result of intellectual rebellion on the part of their founders against their own personal karma.

"The spiritual community of the enlightened will expound

the real democracy of the new republic wherein the nobility of life in its God-intended expression is its own acknowledged reward. No one will expect to be given honors or rights he does not deserve; neither will anyone expect to deny to others their just opportunity to expand their understanding, test their spirituality, or pursue life, liberty and true happiness to the fullest.

Blocks to the Brotherhood's Service

"It is to the complete achievement of these goals that the Great White Brotherhood is dedicated. The powers of the Brotherhood have been limited only in appearance or outer expression by mankind's oft-expressed proneness to misuse free will and ignore the advice of the Brotherhood.

"The same limitations that operate among men on earth to prevent or hinder man from perceiving and becoming the full manifestation of God as impersonal love in action are also present in mass misqualified thought and feeling as opposition to the universal benign intent of the Great White Brotherhood. Were this not so, the perfect world would long ago have been outpictured in human society.

"One of the principal challenges the Brotherhood itself faces is the training of chelas who will accept the responsibility of serving the eternal purposes while seeking individual perfection and spiritual victory. This cooperation between heaven and earth increases the Brotherhood's sphere of influence upon earth, bringing into manifestation at the earliest possible date more and more of the world plan of the Brotherhood, which is ever one with the universal will of God or good. . . .

Branches of the Great White Brotherhood

"The Great White Brotherhood has many branches—some devoted to spiritual science and some to material science, others to the arts, culture, music, sculpture, architecture and community planning. Jurisprudence, both human and divine, are operative under beloved Portia and the Great Karmic Board; the governments of the world, under beloved El Morya; science and medicine, under beloved Hilarion; and each of the many fields of endeavor, both human and divine, is supervised by a branch of the Great White Brotherhood.... "

Membership and Initiation

Chananda continues: "Mundane government seems wholly logical, for on earth it represents the vesting of power in the hands of the few who act for the many in a supposedly just and correct manner. Those who have thought much on the governing aspects of divinity and who have pondered the truism 'Order is heaven's first law' should have no difficulty in accepting divine government.

"They understand that it emanates from the Godhead in a wholly impersonal manner, aided and abetted in its earthly administration by illumined Ascended Beings. These immortal beings, having been cut free from worldly thought and mortal expression, joyously remain connected with the earth and its people in order to serve the causes of divine purpose.

"This august body of the faithful is wholly constructive and may also include spiritually illumined unascended beings dedicated to the will of God, who serve with and under the direction and radiation of those magnificent Ascended and Cosmic Beings who are consecrated to the fulfillment of the divine plan on earth.

"The Great White Brotherhood is wholly dedicated to the use of consecrated energies drawn from God through the conscious efforts of the Ascended Masters in behalf of mankind, implemented by the willing cooperation of those unascended beings who both knowingly and unknowingly cooperate with the divine intent.

"In the truest sense the Great White Brotherhood is a fraternity of the Spirit, recognizing and embracing the Fatherhood of God and the brotherhood of man, which operates with divine authority, divine recognition, foreknowledge and absolute authorization of the Deity.

"The Great White Brotherhood initiates many members. Yet none of them can ever admit to or boast of this membership. However, specially trained workers are occasionally authorized to reveal specific information to certain advanced or prospective chelas in order to accomplish a special purpose.

"Membership in the Great White Brotherhood cannot be purchased at any price, nor can anyone who is unworthy be admitted to its sacred conclaves. By invitation men can rise to this high honor—yet many notable figures of the world, unknown to their outer consciousness, are inner initiates of this beloved fraternity.

"Cooperation with the Brotherhood can be fostered through membership in the Keepers of the Flame Fraternity, which is chartered and authorized by the Great White Brotherhood in accordance with Ascended Master light and love.

"From such faithful cooperating lifestreams as those who remain steadfast in this high calling, the Ascended Masters are able, as the result of proximity and training, to draw initiates and servants of hierarchy to further the mighty cause (when these show themselves readied and approved unto God). [The Keepers of the Flame Lessons are] designed, then, to help all to keep the flame....

"Initiation into the Brotherhood today is somewhat different than it was in ages past. Long ago the would-be chela was taken to Luxor, Heliopolis, Lhasa or elsewhere and given trials of great endurance involving both physical and spiritual tests. The rigors of these trials almost defy imagination, and many of the would-be chelas fell short of passing the mark.

"Those who did not are among the immortals. Today, however, changing times, new methods of communication and transportation, and other factors have altered many old conditions, and new spiritual techniques have been evolved just as material methods have changed.

"Therefore, most of the students living in the present Aquarian age are being given their initiations in the outer world. Karmic events are (so to speak) altered, and friends, relatives, associates and even the man in the street become the instruments through which tests come.

"This makes it necessary for mankind and especially the would-be disciple to be extremely vigilant, for one never knows just when a vital and conclusive test may be in the offing. However, let me emphasize that you must not permit this statement to cause you to become apprehensive. Just be diligent to behave as a Christ, remembering his words 'Inasmuch as ye have done it unto the least of these my brethren, ye have done it unto me.'

"If you will really follow this you may well pass with flying colors any test that the Brotherhood sends for your perfection, admonishment and initiation into the highest spiritual brotherhoood—the Great White Brotherhood—the fraternity of beloved Jesus, Kuthumi, El Morya, Djwal Kul, beloved Lanto, Kuan Yin, Mother Mary, beloved Serapis Bey, Paul the Venetian, and every Ascended and Cosmic Being.

"To this aspire! To this calling be dedicated! There is much, much more to the Great White Brotherhood than either tongue or pen could tell."[8]

Anthropomorphic Gods

The Goddess of Liberty tells us: "The Masters of Wisdom, in their great outreach in every age and at the beginning of the twentieth century, have not neglected to inform mankind about the reality of the Brotherhood. The cloak of religion—which has smothered rather than swaddled mankind's beginnings in Truth—has masked the face of creative expansion, set brother against brother, absorbed mankind's energies in fruitless struggle, and weakened the plan of the Brotherhood for the unity of this age.

"As we inspired the leadership of Abraham, Noah, Moses and other great patriarchs, as we spoke through Zarathustra, Apollonius of Tyana and Jesus, as we released holy wisdom to Socrates, Plato and Emerson, so did we come through Madame Helena Petrovna Blavatsky in *Isis Unveiled* and *The Secret Doctrine.*

"We have also released our instruction through other adherents of divine Truth, both metaphysical and occult, until the occult law was set aside and the pure passion of the flames of liberty and truth was unleashed in the early 1930s.

"Man—caught in the miasma of his separatist dream, deigning to be fooled—has created a thousand foolish splinters that have taken him from the Truth center of his being. It is not that the germ of reality and Truth is not active within the many spiritual organizations upon earth. It is simply that individuals do not grasp Truth when they find it, but prefer instead to form their own anthropomorphic God (a god made in their own image) and to embrace concepts that are foreign to reality."[9]

The Masters sponsor advanced activities to bring progressive Truth to mankind. The Great White Brotherhood originally sponsored the early Christian Church and most of the religions of the world. And the Masters of Wisdom knew full well that with the passing of time crystallization would occur in the tenets of the faith vouchsafed to the founding fathers. They knew this crystallization would occur through the consciousness of those who inherited the letter without receiving the inspiration of the Spirit.

Progressive Revelation Denied

Today many religionists throughout the world are in the bonds of ignorance and the gall of bitterness, opposing the very plans that hold their greatest hope. Ministers and priests cry out against the Truth—supposing that because their traditions are long-enduring, they must be divinely ordained and therefore infallible. They deny progressive revelation, citing as proof the numerous little splinter groups and purveyors of psychism who mimic and pretend to be true prophets of God.

The Great Divine Director says: "It is difficult for individuals to understand just how others can be so gullible about spiritual things as to pin their faith on that which is obviously fraudulent. I do not think that the world is full of frauds, as men might imagine, but rather do I know that it is full of individuals who are often manipulated by forces beyond their ken."[10]

Those who accuse the true prophets of God of being tools of the devil have been tricked by the devil himself. Jesus said, "By their fruits ye shall know them,"[11] and it has been well said that the fruit falls not far from the parent tree.

The release of Truth is not just a series of words, concepts or ideas. It is a vibratory action that reaches up to the Godhead and brings the crystal flowing stream of that action into human affairs. There it is diluted by some, diverted by others, and delighted in by those whose love for freedom and Truth has raised their own vibrations to the place where they partake of its sparkling effervescence and absorb every bit that comes their way.

Let men seek understanding rather than vengeance. Let them examine the fabric of their own thought, and let them also examine the thoughts of the Ascended Masters. Let them remember that they did not come by their present state of awareness of ideas, ideologies and religious views in the short space of a day or a year.

The "Push-Pull" System of Seeking God

Saint Germain suggests an approach to spirituality that relies on both heavenly and earthly activities: "There are many schools of thought in the world concerning spiritual progress— how to make it and how to keep it. Not recognizing the reason for the existence of these different approaches to spirituality, some chelas become confused.

"They do not realize that outside of those organizations that are directly connected with the Great White Brotherhood, there are few that offer a balanced understanding of all of the many facets of the divine expression. Let me then remind those who are sincere to pay special heed to the tenets of the Great White Brotherhood.

"Some schools advocate the development of spiritual consciousness, indicating to their students that this spiritual consciousness will ultimately become so powerful as to cause all negative and baneful influences to drop off from them as overly ripe fruit from a tree.

"Other schools advocate the need for purification, indicating to their chelas that by purifying themselves from the elements of human creation they will naturally find their way back to God. In one sense I would call the former a 'push' system and the latter a 'pull' system.

"Now, let me say that while good exists in both systems, we advocate the use of both rather than one. We believe the 'push-pull' system of seeking God to be the best system of all. Let men recognize the need to purify their worlds from their own human creation, but let them also recognize the need to invoke the assistance of heaven on their behalf. And through attunement with that blessed heaven and the consciousness of the Ascended Masters, let them invoke all beauty unfolding within them here below as Above."[12]

The Higher Law Is Expressed in Many Ways

A great emissary from Venus, speaking at a conference of the Indian Council of the Great White Brotherhood, commented on how the Brotherhood uses many forms of religion to channel the energies of God to his creation:

"Theologians and mortal men of earth often seem incapable of differentiating between a stepped-down release of the Spirit of God and a higher release of the same Spirit. Let them understand the parallel example in their own expression: 'The wind is tempered to the shorn lamb.'

"The blessedness of Almighty God, his Spirit, and the Spirit of his 'sun radiance' (the Christ consciousness, charged with all infinite illumination and the capacity to alter conditions for mankind) abides at the highest levels of the Godhead. It is one with the Father but descends into the very heart of the earth to contact the most primitive and elemental individuals, manifesting diversely to each level in order that each one might derive the greatest benefit that the Great Law could pass to him according to his capacity to receive.

"Be not then entangled in the yoke of bondage that differing religious opinions sometimes bring about. Understand, blessed ones of earth, that many manifestations of God are necessary in order to reach the various levels of understanding and progress. There is no enmity between one manifestation of

God and another. There is only the outreach of God farther from his heart, designed and intended to reach and save that which is lost."[13]

The Brotherhood Encourages Practical Spirituality

The Goddess of Liberty offers this advice to those who would put their highest aspirations into practice on earth: "All religion that has had its origin in the spirit of Truth ought (1) to bring to mankind a greater awareness of divine potential, (2) to serve as a bond of union 'twixt the Brotherhood of light and unascended man, and (3) to illumine mankind as to the pitfalls of worldly living.

"These pitfalls are not absent from the spiritual path, not by any means. No immunity has been guaranteed the advancing chela. Indeed, those who consider themselves wise in the teaching are expected to be more alert than those sweet young disciples whose laughing hearts first come to the newness of divine understanding.

"The business of living is a serious business, but it can be indulged with a steadied merriment and a bubbling joy. The mists that have clouded the minds of men must be dispersed. The sun of hope must rise as many hands unite to pluck the harmonic strings of genuine brotherhood.

"The sons of liberty will rally, and the world will know the mounting passion of hearts who love freedom. These love freedom enough to hold high her torch, to look 'round about them and to pick up the debris that the flame will gladly transmute. No service is too lowly for these. For they follow in the wake of angelic vows, offering eternal service to God.

"Does a humble heart need assistance? They serve. Must a thankless task be done? They do. Shall a seemingly archaic matter require study? They apply their minds. Is organization needed? They organize. Whatever the exigency, they reach up to the abundance of God, magnetize it, and offer it in the service of the light."[14]

We wish to point out that dedicated servants of the Great White Brotherhood must beware of organizations that profess to follow the teachings of the Brotherhood, but whose means in obtaining that goal are tyrannical. The student must be careful to examine not only the lofty ideals and the aims of such organizations but also their modus operandi.

Is the individual enslaved in order that the goal of brotherhood be realized? Is he deprived of initiations or tests of self-mastery by compensations, welfare payments or social dividends that he has not earned? Is his initiative to develop his Christ-potential blunted by a superimposed equality that does not take into account the Law that as a man sows, so shall he reap—that each one's talents must first be multiplied before he can receive the dividends of a wise investment of his life's energies?

World Service

Do not think that the spiritually elect are not needed in the political affairs of the nations, for the God-government of the earth is among the highest callings of the servant-sons of God. It is time for the children of the light to come forth to take their place in the so-called mundane affairs of the world. For the Great White Brotherhood teaches that every act done in the name of God is sacred, and inasmuch as we have done it unto the least of these our brethren, we have done it unto the Christ. Public service in his name is one of the greatest callings upon earth at this hour of world crisis.

Opposing this service is the rebellious consciousness that seeks to keep the people ignorant—ignorant of reality, of their true Source, of the goal of life that is the ascension, and of the individual's true dignity. That dignity derives from his kinship with God. He is a son of God; the threefold flame blazes within his heart; he is destined to be a king and a priest unto God.

John said to try the spirits to see whether they be of God.[15] Let us, then, try the motives of those who would enlist our energies in a supposedly righteous cause. Let us ask the question: "Are the means worthy of the ends?" And let us never accept the philosophy that the end justifies the means.

Let the children of the sun beware of the philosophies of the manipulators in government, in politics, in social work, in education, in art and in music. For all that tears down the Christ consciousness is unworthy of perpetuation. But all that builds the golden-age civilization should receive the loyal, prayerful attention of everyone who is homeward bound.

Spiritual Education

During the periods of great darkness upon the planet, which have been present to a greater or lesser degree in every age, the activities of the Great White Brotherhood have been driven underground because of the intense reaction of the darkness in the hearts of the people to the light of the descending Christ consciousness.

Through a renaissance of art and culture, the release of the music of the spheres through great composers, and an infusion of illumination's flame, the Great White Brotherhood has sought to pave the way for an increasing expression of the Christ light. But that which has been accomplished on the physical plane and in the outer consciousness has not been enough to secure the blessings of light for posterity and to hold back the forward movement of the forces of darkness.

Therefore, in caring for the spiritual needs of mankind, the

Brotherhood has found it necessary to utilize many forms of communion and education. These include what might be termed "co-education," whereby the soul of man, apart from the mortal form while the body sleeps at night, becomes correctly informed concerning the great truths of the universe. This co-education is carried on in the Masters' physical and etheric retreats, which have been maintained throughout the world for centuries.

The concepts that are taught there are unacceptable to the domain of mortal reason in the daylight consciousness—simply because teachers, friends, companions and circumstances have already set up a matrix in the person's mind based upon human concepts, bereft of the wisdom contained in the record of pure God Truth.

Thus the majority among mankind do not retain the memory of their experiences at inner levels. Nevertheless, an imprint of the events is made upon the mental and emotional bodies, and little by little the memories of the instruction received come to the fore of the outer mind. The benefits conferred to the soul, which are recorded in the subconscious, come to the surface of consciousness.

More advanced initiates are invited to attend the council meetings of the Great White Brotherhood, including the Darjeeling and Indian Councils, the Council of the Royal Teton, and various committee meetings that the Masters heading the branches of the Brotherhood's endeavors hold.

These meetings are not attended in the flesh, but by means of spiritual projection or the projection of consciousness. (This is never astral projection or an astral experience.) Some of the more advanced devotees are able to participate in these conclaves with the full conscious awareness of the outer mind, even though they attend with only their subtle or finer bodies.

Others who are not allowed to attend these meetings may tune in to them just as we tune in through radio and television to events that are happening at a distance. Those who can attune to the vibratory rate of the Masters' consciousness can in this manner receive the higher teachings and participate in the council meetings from afar.

Special Training

On occasion, unascended lifestreams are taken in their physical bodies to the retreats of the Brotherhood, to be trained for special service in the world of form that requires superhuman strength and certain disciplines that can only be imparted to the unascended initiate in the retreats. Jesus was taken into the retreat in Luxor and into the Temple of the Blue Lotus prior to his three-year ministry.

This rare privilege is also given to others who have not yet transmuted all of their karma. They use the experience to help them render valiant service to life. They receive the same assistance that was given in the Cave of Light to Godfré, Rex, Nada, Bob and Pearl, whom Saint Germain sponsored through the "I AM" activity.[16] Through this sponsorship their four lower bodies are purified and aligned so they might be the immaculate receptacles of the Christ consciousness.

When this dispensation is accorded to worthy chelas, their remaining service to life is magnificently accomplished, because their consciousness becomes the perfect focal point in the world of form for the release of the entire Spirit of the Great White Brotherhood. Miracles (demonstrations of alchemy) and the control of natural forces and elemental life become the mark of those who are so blessed by the opportunity of being "perfected" prior to their final initiation and ascension in the light.

Protecting the Brotherhood's Focuses

Since all that is on the physical plane has an etheric counterpart, the physical focuses of the Brotherhood already have an etheric counterpart either intermeshing with the focus or located directly above it in the atmosphere. Where both still exist, unascended devotees carry on at the physical level that which the Ascended Masters are carrying on at the etheric level and also in the higher octaves of light.

Down through the ages, many of the physical retreats of the Brotherhood have been closed as civilizations crumbled around them and ignorant masses desecrated the shrines. Others were closed before they were destroyed, for the hierarchs of the retreats felt an imminent threat to the physical focus and the ancient relics guarded there.

During the Chinese Communists' ravaging of Tibet since the 1950s, some of the sacred temples of the Brotherhood there have been closed and the sacred relics transported to temples of the Brotherhood located in other parts of the world. In other cases, the temples were sealed within mountains or within the earth itself, preventing any possibility of intrusion by those whose consciousness is unprepared to enter the Holy of Holies.

If it is impossible to save the accoutrements of a retreat and the entrances cannot be sealed, the etheric counterpart of the focus is raised to a point in the atmosphere above the physical structure and the forces of nature are employed through cataclysmic action to destroy the remains.

Inasmuch as the etheric counterpart of the physical is more real than the physical (the etheric being the cause and the physical the effect), when the enlightenment of civilization once again reaches a point where it is safe to precipitate in form that which exists as etheric pattern, the Brothers and Sisters of the retreat so direct it.

The Brotherhood's Retreats
Are Strategically Located

The retreats, temples and focuses of the Masters are scientifically located upon the planetary body at certain key
points in the design of the mandala. Their positions are calculated for the greatest release of light to the evolutions evolving
here. All of the retreats act as receiving and sending stations for
the light released in all of the other retreats upon the planetary
body and for the light sent from near and distant stars, and
from the flaming Yod in the Great Hub.

The light emitted from the retreats bounces back and forth
between them in magnetic waves. This interaction of the light
produces the resonance of a cosmic tone, the sound of the
great amen—the Om—which can be heard with the inner ear.

This cosmic keynote bathes the earth, the nature kingdom
and mankind in the vibratory action of the sacred Word of
creation, which means literally "I AM" or "God is the great
amen." By this we know that every man can become one with
the vibration of the lost Word.

From time to time representatives of the false hierarchy,
working through misguided though well-meaning channels
in the world of form, have released the information that certain
of the Masters' retreats have been moved. A few have even
proclaimed that the retreats have been moved to a position
above the location of their own organizations. These rumors
have caused a great commotion among some devotees.

Concerned with the protection of the faithful, beloved El
Morya wrote a letter to the students to clarify the position of
the Great White Brotherhood on this subject: "Never will we
withdraw our support from any sincere, God-loving individual.
Neither will we permit anyone to usurp authority with im-
punity and attempt to present to mankind the false premise

that the Ascended Master retreats, which are fixed through love and devotion poured out for millennia, are to be removed from their etheric locations above the landed areas of the earth where they have been sustained by the angelic hosts and have served the needs of the entire planet for so long.

"It is a fact that the entire sphere of the etheric mesh in which the etheric retreats are located can (and sometimes does) rotate independently of the earth at a speed far exceeding the earth's own rotational norm. Thereby there is created a harmonic tone combining the musical keys of the many Ascended Master retreats. These manifest as a wondrous chord of pure love—somewhat in the manner of a child's musical top.

"Therefore, since these retreats were scientifically positioned by the Brotherhood according to Cosmic Law, it would be in violation of that Law and indeed wholly unnecessary to disturb their wonderful etheric pattern in order to convey a blessing to any part of the earth or to any person thereon.

"To do so would be to upset the delicate magnetic field of the entire earth, and this would serve no useful purpose. After all, blessed ones, if the North and South Poles were to be put at the equator, would this not disturb the balance of the earth? Remember that by mighty light rays we can and do reach every part of the earth and expand the light within men's hearts wherever they are.

"Inasmuch as the retreats are visited by mankind in their finer bodies, it does not matter where on earth these retreats are located from the standpoint of availability and blessings conferred to all of life....

"Our retreats remain inviolate for cosmic purposes. We may from time to time establish new centers that will one day become, by intelligent effort and service, mighty focuses of love. And we have, on rare occasions, moved a flame or reestablished it, by mighty light rays to affect a nation for good."[17]

You Are Welcome to Study at the Brotherhood's Retreats

The etheric cities together with the following retreats are open the year 'round to qualified and deserving chelas of the Ascended Masters for study and meditation. According to the chart of their birth cycle (the hierarchy of the sun to which they have been assigned), as well as the ray on which they are serving, the Lords of Karma assign the disciples to certain retreats during certain periods of the year.

A number of years ago the false concept was released that only one or several retreats were open each month and that all students of the Masters should therefore go to that specific retreat during that month. This was another attempt of the sinister force to deprive mankind of the full complement of assistance that was and always has been available to unascended mankind.

All the retreats contribute to the release of light and to the grids and forcefields that comprise the hierarchical mandala sustaining and balancing the action of the threefold flame of the Christ consciousness on the planet. This necessarily entails the participation of the students in the action of all the flames of all the retreats that are open each month.

Before retiring at night, the student should call to his God Presence and his guardian angel to take him in his finer bodies to one of the following retreats. Or he may simply ask to be taken to the retreat to which he has been assigned for that particular cycle of his evolution.

The retreats of the Great White Brotherhood now receiving students [c. 1972—Ed.] are the Royal Teton, the retreats of beloved John and Eriel, the Temple of Faith at Banff, the Temple of Illumination at Lake Titicaca, the Ascension Temple, the Cathedral of Nature, the Cave of Symbols, the Château de

Liberté, the Temple of Comfort, the retreat of Hercules and Amazonia, the Temple of Peace, the Temple of Purity, the Resurrection Temple, the Temple of the Maltese Cross over the House of Rakoczy in the Carpathian Mountains, the Temple of Good Will, the Cave of Light, the Temple of Truth, the Temple of Mercy, the Tibetan retreat of Djwal Kul, and the retreats of the Master of Paris and the Queen of Light.[18]

Calls to beloved Archangel Michael and Mighty Astrea before retiring will ensure the soul's safe passage through the astral belt to the higher octaves of light—and also a safe return. If the student experiences frequent occurrences of discordant dreams, it is an indication that he is not passing through the lower levels of consciousness like the clean cut of the blade of a knife. He should redouble his efforts to decree during the day, before retiring at night and during periods when he is awakened by discomfiting vibrations during the night.

Impersonators of the Ascended Masters

Impostors, false hierarchs, black magicians and masquerading entities have imitated the teachings of the Great White Brotherhood. Every Ascended Master is imitated by one or more dark souls who go forth in his name to release fraudulent material to unascended lifestreams.

These impersonators of the Masters are very clever. They are able to imitate the Masters' vibrations, their etheric patterns and their appearance so well that only an expert is able by the grace of God to distinguish the synthetic image from the real image. Because the language and even the tone of voice of the impostor closely resembles that of the Master whom he imitates, the Great Divine Director gives this practical advice:

"Call upon your own Divine Presence and wait upon the Word of the LORD. Live closely and identify with the precepts of holy Truth that bring to the doorstep of every man the understanding of the full measure of his responsibility to his brother, made in the image of God, to whom he ought to offer the best that is within himself, owing direct allegiance to his great God-being.

"Where there is a dichotomy between the counsels of that great divine being and those of another individual or group of individuals, the attention should always flow first to the Divine Presence and then to the Ascended Masters' realm for the resolving of the difficulty. Light always begets light to nourish and regenerate, whereas darkness may indeed masquerade as intellectual blindness, which refuses to accept the Truth of that which it cannot see concretely defined.

"Every doctrine that is rooted in sinister strategies and seeks to cater to the mortal mind of man or to pamper his ego (leading him to believe that he is connected with some 'outer source' that will keep him informed as to what is happening around the cosmic corner) is simply an activity designed to please the little self and to enlarge the boundaries of that self.

"Cosmic magnification, which is the fruit of divine sowing, does not seek to embellish the ego nor to make the individual feel that he is above his fellowmen. Rather does it seek the identification of the individual with cosmic resources, which enlarge the borders of man's perception by the light of divine Truth."[19]

The Correct Use of the Ascended Masters' Names

The Great Divine Director has also released instruction on the correct use of the Ascended Masters' names: "The Word of God by which heaven and earth were framed was the eternally resonant voice of the Logos, but in the world of form it became drowned by many human voices and many human words. The ringing statement 'There is none other name under heaven given among men, whereby we must be saved' clearly showed the feeling of the early apostles of the Christian Church with reference to the sacredness attached to the divine name."[20]

The Great Divine Director explains that the names of the Ascended Masters are keys to their electronic pattern, to their consciousness and vibration. As each letter in the alphabet keys to a cosmic frequency and release, the combination of letters in an Ascended Master's name constitutes his personal keynote.

In the case of well-known Masters such as Jesus Christ—whose name has been called upon by devotees for centuries—a great momentum of light has coalesced around the name, adding the devotion of unascended mankind to the momentum of light released by the name "Jesus." So powerful is this name of the Son of God that it may be used to the present hour to cast out demons and entities.

Disregarding these facts, various channels in embodiment have allowed themselves to be duped by ambitious and calculating minds who, speaking from the lower astral planes, have proclaimed that Jesus Christ is no longer to be called Jesus, but another name. Likewise, these forces have announced that the names of the Great Divine Director, Saint Germain, Cyclopea and Lord Maitreya should be changed.

The names given in each case were those of impostors who had long desired to usurp the office of these magnificent Cosmic Beings. Dangerous black magicians are they, who trick innocent victims into calling upon their names while offering adoration to God in prayer, meditation and decrees. These blackguards then take the pure energies of the students and use them to perpetuate the black conspiracy upon the planet.

At other times inaccurate channels have received the information that not only the names, but also the offices of such magnificent beings as the Lord Maha Chohan and Paul the Venetian have been changed, or that certain Masters such as beloved El Morya have gone on to cosmic service and are therefore no longer available to answer the calls of unascended mankind.

Concerning this subject the Great Divine Director says: "The Beloved Master Paul the Venetian remains the Chohan of the third ray of Divine Love, for his service to life in that office is far from finished. And the Lord Maha Chohan remains with all of the divine cosmic honor as simply 'The Maha Chohan,' which means 'The Great Lord.'

"As his consciousness and power soar in the service of the light and for mankind, the power of his office is not diminished, but transcends itself again and again, illumining and bringing release from the pains of wrong thought and feeling to many among mankind. . . .

"The power of God has for centuries been vested in the names of these Ascended Masters, and to use other names does not increase the power of God or the power of Truth. For if these new names that mankind have tacked on to the Ascended Masters are called upon, they key the disciple into the vibratory action of an impostor.

"Thus the disciple, without realizing it, is putting the funnel of his attention into a cesspool and the mire of jaded consciousness, while at the same time ignorantly denying the power of the Lords of light (whom mankind have been taught to call upon from their mothers' knees in some cases, and in others from the date of their illumination).

"Blessed ones, be not deceived, for the scriptures have clearly stated that there would arise false Christs and false prophets who would show great signs and wonders, insomuch that, if it were possible, they would deceive the very elect.[21]

"The great power of Divine Love, which is in the Ascended Masters' octave, remains fixed there. When the key of the correct name of the Master is used and the attention flows to that

Master, it will always return the peace and blessing of that individual Son of God into the world of the seeker.

"When individuals in ignorance call upon other names and their hearts are pure, it does not always mean that they will experience some negative outpouring of which they are consciously aware. But in reality there is always a diminution of the light flow into their worlds. In some, there have been awful obsessions created and the infestation of entities into their worlds, because they have been thrown off the path of Truth by calling upon others who are in reality not Masters of light but impostors of the black brotherhood masquerading as angels of light. 'And no marvel; for Satan himself is transformed into an angel of light.'[22]

"In him who has said 'I AM is my name,' all beings merge into the great light. But they retain the new name that they have been given by God, which is in reality the old name that no man knoweth save he who has received it."[23]

In the charts on the hierarchy that we have released in the first book of this series, we have given the correct names of the Elohim, the Archangels and the Chohans. The Great Divine Director has promised that when the time is right for greater clarification on the names of the members of hierarchy, it will be given.

He promised the students that the time would come for the revelation of such corrections as were necessary for the maximum release of light from the Great White Brotherhood to their unascended devotees. Let none then be dismayed but all move forward in a greater consciousness of the Truth, which by the action of the two-edged sword cleaves asunder the real from the unreal.

El Morya's Fifteen-Point Program

Beloved El Morya once outlined a fifteen-point program of assistance that the councils of the Brotherhood had determined to release to mankind. These points sum up the purposes of the Brotherhood through the ages. We include them in this chapter so that those who desire to place their hands firmly in the hands of the Brothers in White may understand specifically what they may do to further the divine plan for the earth and invoke the assistance that the heavenly hosts deem most important in this hour of world need.

El Morya writes: "Who can deny the needs of this hour or of humanity? Who should? It is our earnest desire to render the following assistance to mankind individually and collectively, as they are able to respond to the ministrations of the heavenly hosts:

1. to step up the level of individual service in order to provide for greater clarity of understanding to men of lesser comprehension;

2. to set forth in a most desirable manner the higher teachings of Cosmic Law for those who are able to grasp them;

3. to create more stable ties with the hierarchy through our cosmic outposts in the world of men;

4. to introduce new levels of integrity, justice and faith in government and business, and in religious, scientific and artistic endeavors;

5. to amplify the power of godly vision among men to assist those who have seen or experienced little of the heavenly kingdom;

6. to develop the spiritual nature of all peoples in order that they may experience greater joy in carrying out the will of God wherever and whenever they are called upon to serve;

7. to sustain faith in those who yet must walk by it;

8. to meet the spiritual needs of mankind at all levels of consciousness;

9. to promote peace and understanding in order to accelerate the manifestation of cosmic purpose;

10. to utilize renewed interest in extrasensory perception and matters of the Spirit in order to direct the seeker toward the unfolding of his latent divinity rather than involvement in a search for the phenomenal;

11. to elucidate further to mankind upon the great story of the cosmic hierarchy;

12. to build mighty pools of reserve energies as reservoirs of spiritual power that can be used by the disciples of the Ascended Masters in their service to mankind and for the blessing of all life directly from the retreats of the Ascended Masters;

13. to secure new dispensations from the Karmic Board that will feed these energy pools and embodied individuals connected with the hierarchy with sufficient power and cosmic know-how to externalize the plan for the year;

14. to encourage all—even the downtrodden—to keep high their faith in the ultimate outpicturing of the glory of God, right while perceiving the absolute necessity to counteract the ignorant manifestations of mankind involved in their excessive materialism, the use of psychedelic and other types of recreational drugs, dissonant music and art forms, and vain pleasure-seeking to their own hurt; and

15. to integrate the whole man in accordance with the original divine plan."[24]

Chapter 2

Ascended and Unascended Masters

*There comes a time when man
passes beyond the pale of that which his
own experience patterns can teach him.
Then the immortals stand ready, even as
they do while he is still learning the lessons
of earth, to help him expand in every facet
of his endeavors, whether human or divine.*

SAINT GERMAIN

 # Ascended and
Unascended Masters

MANY STUDENTS OF THE OCCULT, of mysticism and of spiritual law become involved in a search for the masters. To sit at the feet of a master is a goal to which many aspire. They feel that if they can contact a living master, their own victory will be assured—while not a few aspire to be the master of other men.

These seek to gather around themselves those to whom they can give advice, while often they themselves are unable to manifest their own victory over the very conditions from which their students seek deliverance. Of these Peter says, "While they promise them liberty, they themselves are the servants of corruption."[1] Thus many have found that the pathway to the masters is not all that they thought it would be. And they have returned to their own hearth, the spiritual quest unfulfilled.

Nevertheless, there are indeed what we may call true unascended masters, just as there are Ascended Masters. Unascended masters are those who have attained a degree of mastery but who, for various reasons, have not taken their ascension. Ascended Masters are those who have mastered life on earth, fulfilled their divine plan, balanced a minimum of 51 percent of their karma and taken their ascension.

As we compare the joint services of Ascended Masters and unascended masters, let us define the term "mastery." Mastery is the state of having power of command, expert skill or proficiency, in a given field, area of knowledge or discipline. Now, there are masters of science, of art, of music and of the professions. Yet these are not necessarily masters of life and death.

In our consideration of masters we mean those who have attained mastery over themselves. These are they who have learned to govern their energies and to discipline their thoughts and feelings. They have mastery over the cycles of life and are mastered by neither the tides of their returning karma nor the tides of the mass consciousness (with the exception, perhaps, of a narrow margin of their personal lives that may require the attention of the Master of masters). These are indeed unascended masters.

Many today consider Ramakrishna to have been such a one. Others consider the great Master Babaji of the Himalayas and his sister Mataji to be unascended masters. Masters they are indeed, who have foregone the ritual of the ascension in order to serve what is known as the bodhisattva ideal.

Traits of True Unascended Masters

We turn now to the writings of the Ascended Master Saint Germain to examine the differences between Ascended Masters and the unascended masters of the Far East:

"[Unascended masters] are adepts who are called masters, yet they have not taken the ritual of the ascension. Some of these, after having entered nirvana or a lesser state of adeptship, return in consciousness to the physical form. Here they recharge their flesh forms in preparation for greater service; nonetheless, for various reasons, they do not go through the ascension process.

"A rare few among the unascended masters have been able to perpetuate life in the same body over long periods, thereby continuing the opportunity to balance a great deal of karma and becoming in the eyes of many as gods in the flesh.

"It is also true that some of these find it impossible to demonstrate the mastery of retaining life in one body. Therefore, they do reembody from time to time, while continuing to abide in the nirvanic state during intervals in their long journey toward higher mastership and the ascension.

"The powers that these unascended masters demonstrate are sometimes phenomenal, but this does not set them above those who are in the ascended state. All should know that soul progress is the real goal, not the exhibition of power in one or more of its forms (although such powers are often evidence of soul development). Also, seekers should beware of false adepts whose control of substance is used for self-aggrandizement and destructive intent. Often these put forth an appearance of good, but in reality they are self-oriented.

"It is true that by the exercise of their sovereign free will, men can elect to fulfill their evolution in any manner and by any means that they deem acceptable. But all should be apprised that we who have overcome the world point the way to the ascended state as the highest state to which anyone can aspire.

"From this state mankind do not fall back again into a form of lesser consciousness, and from this state a permanent entrance into nirvana and even higher aspects of God consciousness can be developed and retained as infinite progress is made.

"It is known that many of the Eastern masters do not summon enough of the divine will to enable them to pass all of the required initiations in order to transcend the flesh. Yet it cannot be denied that they frequently manifest high states of consciousness. To be associated with them as a disciple is not without responsibility, nor is it without limitation.

"It is understood by those who enter into the guru-chela relationship that there will be a certain involvement in karmic conditions that as an auric net surround all unascended mankind, whether they be advanced teachers or their pupils. For without karma no one can remain unascended without special dispensation from the Karmic Board.

"The benign aspects of their karma, which involve service, instruction and healing, enable unascended masters to confer definite benefits upon their chelas. These in turn can be relieved of varying amounts of their own negative karma as the master himself takes on (in part) the balancing of his disciples' karma.

"Let us also consider the benefits of becoming a chela of the Ascended Masters. The Ascended Masters may have a residue of karma that they must balance from the ascended octave, but being free from the karma-making round, they do not continue to make personal karma.

"It is true that Ascended Masters have at various times taken on mankind's karma and that they have assisted them in working out their problems in the same manner as do those whom we have termed unascended masters.

"But the assistance, blessed ones, that can be rendered to a chela of the Ascended Masters is always of the highest form. Never does it involve any form of danger whatsoever, except it be the danger of not accepting the opportunity for eternal life that the Master offers.

"Therefore, I would warn all students of light: you have a certain responsibility for the professions you make in the name of your teacher, whether he be ascended or unascended. For is it not written, 'By thy words thou shalt be justified, and by thy words thou shalt be condemned'?[2] That which is said incorrectly in the name of one vested with a high spiritual office carries the weight of karma for that office, which is always greater for the illumined than for the unillumined. . . .

"In the same manner, if any teacher give out false doctrine, he is responsible to those who are injured by his error until they attain their ascension in the light. This is why Ascended Masters have karma. Many times just a few erroneous concepts that crept into an otherwise accurate spiritual document have caused the downfall of a sincere student.

"Thus, the Master who has gained his ascension for the good he has done must continue to assist those who have been hindered on their journey by the wrong he unwittingly committed while unascended.

"There are attached to the earth many great beings who are obliged to serve here until all imperfect markings that they made while unascended are erased. In the case of one who has served as a world figure, this may be until the last lifestreams win their freedom—or until another Ascended Being offers to hold his office and carry out his service while he goes on to still higher service in the cosmic reaches of infinity."[3]

The Bodhisattva Ideal

Some Ascended Masters have embraced the bodhisattva ideal, vowing to serve the needs of humanity until the last soul is ascended. Kuan Yin, the Goddess of Mercy, has promised to keep the flame of forgiveness on behalf of the evolutions of this planet.

Forgoing cosmic service and advancement in the hierarchical order, she will remain in the Temple of Mercy (located in the etheric plane over the city of Beijing) until all have returned to the heart of God. Such a commitment requires extraordinary dedication even in one who is ascended.

Now, it is neither desirable nor proper that all should pursue this path. In most cases those who do so have earned their ascension but have bypassed it, to provide a focus or an anchor point upon the planet for the higher Mind of God. This is the role of the mahatma, the "great-souled one," who, out of his humble communion with the flame of life, has drawn forth and taken as his own identity the great solar awareness of the consciousness of God.

Such a one becomes a vehicle through which the beautiful currents of divine grace may radiate daily into the world of form. Without such dedicated souls in their midst, millions would be deprived of the divine currents that are vital not only to their existence but also to the balance of forces on the planet.

Ascended Beings can materialize and dematerialize a form that resembles in all aspects the fleshly body of other men but is in effect a spiritual body, a celestial body, not a terrestrial one. Unascended beings cannot.

Yet this is not an absolute criterion, for there are a few men and women who are unascended masters who can also dematerialize and materialize the body. However, most of these operate through a projected consciousness whereby, rather than assembling and disassembling the atoms of a physical body, they create in consciousness a body form that may be projected anywhere in the world and may or may not be seen by others.

Unascended masters are subject to the ills of the flesh, to karma-making circumstances and to the ever-present possibility of being torn down just at the moment when they are ready to be raised up. However, the peril is not so great for these blessed servants as it might first appear, for they do have self-mastery and they are not likely to be caught off guard.

As long as men are embodied in the veil of flesh, there is the possibility that the devotee in an unguarded moment might open the door of his consciousness to inharmony of one kind or another. The karma that might be incurred would have to be balanced before he could once again be restored to the fullness of grace that he had held prior to his becoming enmeshed in mortal thought and feeling.

Requirements for the Ascension

While there are minimal requirements that must be met by a candidate for the ascension, some graduate from earth's school as valedictorians of their class. Others are grateful to have the opportunity to win their freedom from the wheel of birth and death even though they will need to spend many cycles at ascended levels balancing their remaining earthly karma.

To ascend you must

- Balance your threefold flame
- Align your four lower bodies
- Attain mastery on all seven rays
- Achieve mastery over outer conditions
- Fulfill your divine plan
- Transmute your electronic belt
- Raise the Kundalini
- Balance at least 51 percent of your karma

One who has met these requirements but who elects to remain in embodiment, forgoing the ascension in order to serve on earth, need not forfeit his right to progress in the cycles of initiation according to his own level of devotion and attainment. Indeed, he may accelerate the expansion of his solar consciousness while carrying out the assignments of the hierarchy from his unascended state.

Thus it may come to pass that unascended avatars realize a greater degree of spiritual advancement than some newly Ascended Masters. An unascended bodhisattva who has kept the flame on behalf of millions of lifestreams for thousands of

years would certainly be ahead of one who has recently ascended with minimal requirements. Of course, once ascended,
even the least in the kingdom advance rapidly.

Unfettered by the world and the density of human consciousness, Ascended Beings can rise to heights of mastery
much more quickly than those who are burdened with the
responsibilities of serving the needs of the planet from the
unascended state. Nevertheless, the latter acknowledge with
the Christ, "My burden is light."[4]

The Coming of the Avatars and the Order of the Prophets

The coming of such unascended masters into embodiment
is indeed a blessing to the evolutions of the planet, even though
few recognize that such events are taking place. The earth has
received many lifestreams who have pledged to stand, face and
conquer with the mankind of earth every form of error that has
been imposed upon the race.

On February 4, 1962, on the occasion of a conjunction of
planets that astrologers hailed as a cosmic moment, a great number of highly illumined souls were born. Lady Master Venus
said that as these Christs "come to maturity they will assist the
mankind of earth to find their way back to the heart of God."

She explained: "These beings are indeed masters. They are
avatars in descent as was the Christ, and their mission is to
guide the mankind of earth in the Ascended Master age—the
Great Golden Age." The Lady Venus explained that the coming of these souls with their cosmic retinue "precedes the time
when the Ascended Masters themselves shall step from octaves
of light into visible form."[5]

In 1964 nine souls who had attained the Buddhic consciousness came into embodiment at strategic points on the

globe. These had long ago met the requirements for the ascension, but they volunteered to return in the power of the three-times-three to blend their energies with the service of the holy Christ children.

The momentum of light that these Buddhas have magnetized in their auras may be felt for hundreds of miles. When they are in complete attunement with their God Presence (as in meditation or out of the body during sleep), their auras enfold the entire planet in the balancing power of the threefold flame that is sustained by Gautama Buddha in his etheric temple over the Gobi Desert.

The attainment of a Buddha is greater than that of a Christ—that is, the office of Buddha is greater than the office of the Christ in the order of the spiritual hierarchy. Hence many Ascended Masters have not yet reached the Buddhic consciousness. Every Ascended Master would gladly pay homage to the light and mastery of these unascended lifestreams even as the three Magi came to worship the Christ Child (although they themselves were unascended masters).

Not many months after the coming of the Buddhas, one of the nine passed from this world "as a flower cut from the vine,"[6] so lacking in purity were his surroundings. Dauntless in his mission, he volunteered to be born again so that the power of the three-times-three and the pact of the Holy Nine might not be broken.

Thus on April 7, 1969, the Master Jesus announced that that Buddha would return in the land of India, where he was to be born to a blessed couple who had volunteered at inner levels to sponsor and protect his precious lifestream. And so the mission of ascended and unascended masters working hand in hand with humanity moves on, and another chapter in the never-ending Book of Life has a happy ending that promises new beginnings for all.

The Drama of Elijah the Prophet

In our study of ascended and unascended masters, let us now consider the service of Elijah and his great devotion, which led to a most unusual dispensation granted by the Karmic Board in order that he might render further assistance to his beloved pupil Elisha.

Chananda, Chief of the Indian Council of the Great White Brotherhood, refers to this dispensation in a letter to the Keepers of the Flame:

"In the drama of Elijah the prophet, who was caught up into heaven in a chariot of fire, one may learn how the victory of one man's trust and faith in God was able to give him his ascension in the light by the power of the sacred fire. In the case of Elijah, after his ascension he retained his higher vehicle (body) in the octaves of light but descended in part into the being of John the Baptist, who was truly one come 'in the Spirit and power of Elias (Elijah).'[7]

"His is perhaps the one exception, the one case in point, that will prove the divine rule. For in the main when individuals take the initiation of the ascension and are raised back to the heart of God from whence they came, they do not choose to reembody again upon the planet, nor are they chosen for such an activity.

"On the Mount of Transfiguration Moses and Elijah did appear to Jesus—which shows that after the decapitation of John the Baptist at the request of Salome, he did again proceed back to the heart of his ascended state to manifest as Elijah, the Ascended Master.[8]

"Of John the Baptist, because he was an Ascended Being who chose to offer himself for further service to mankind in a very short but important mission, the statement was made, 'Among them that are born of women there hath not risen a greater than John the Baptist.'[9]...

"Jesus himself gave this tribute to John—placing John above himself—for he knew that he (Jesus) must yet pass through the fires of initiation to win the victory that John had already accomplished in his embodiment as Elijah. For it was Jesus embodied as Elisha, the pupil of Elijah, who received the mantle (the cloak of authority) from Elijah and subsequently performed the miracles of healing recorded in the Old Testament.[10]

"The relationship between Elijah and Elisha was of teacher and pupil. Thus Jesus had been initiated in this former embodiment under Elijah in preparation for his great mission in Galilee. It is the desire of every teacher to see his pupil excel and even surpass his own efforts, and therefore John said of Jesus, 'He must increase, but I must decrease.'[11]

"So great was the love of the guru for the chela that he was willing to make the sacrifice of descending to earth from his ascended state to go before his pupil to 'prepare...the way of the Lord.'[12]

"It was the preaching and baptizing of John that paved the way for the coming of the Christ. His was the 'voice of one crying in the wilderness' (in the barrenness of human consciousness, devoid of the light of the Christ). It was John of whom Jesus said that he is 'more than a prophet, for this is he of whom it is written, Behold, I send my messenger before thy face, which shall prepare thy way before thee.'"[13]

Soul Expansion through Love: Techniques of Self-Realization

Devotees of the light who have desired a closer union with God have used various techniques through the ages. These practices have differed from East to West, but always the goal has been the same: the spiritualization of consciousness and the reunion of the soul with the Spirit.

Saint Germain gives further instruction on this subject: "Through various yogic practices individuals enter the state called 'samadhi.' In this state the outer consciousness is suspended in its contact with the senses, and interior bliss is invoked by sustaining contact with the mighty light of God and his inner radiance within man's being.

"Many forms of control are developed over both body and mind through engaging in this practice. The ultimate end thereof is, of course, the attainment of nirvana or the nirvanic state.

"The state of nirvana is one in which the soul, having progressed through the orderly series of initiations available to man upon this planet, enters that cosmic rest whereby one becomes so completely absorbed in his individual I AM Presence that he maintains no contact whatsoever with the outer personality or form.

"Without waiting for the process of the ascension, some individuals pass through various forms of yogic trance into the higher realms. They leave the body temple and even the consciousness itself behind to enter straightway into the highly vibrating center of the Godhead, where all is so still that it seems to be in a state of perpetual rest.

"Dwelling in the peace of the Godhead, some are inclined to remain aloof from the warp and woof of creation. They find complete contentment in God and have no desire to go out from the sun center of his radiance. Thus the nirvanic state, for all practical purposes, becomes the cessation of three-dimensional action.

"I would call to your attention that although Lord Buddha reached this state, he did not permit himself to lose contact with reality as it exists in the denser spheres. Rather, because of the greatness of his love for the world and its people, he responded when he was called back from his nirvanic rest, and he once again descended out of this high initiatic mode into the world of form.

"There he became the hierarch of Shamballa or Lord of the World, enabling Sanat Kumara to return from his long exile upon earth to his planetary home, Venus.[14] (It should be pointed out, however, that Lord Buddha had attained his ascension before entering the state of nirvana and that he chose to enter that state after his ascension.)

"It is definitely possible for individuals who are unascended masters, by reason of their high degree of spiritual attunement, to enter into the nirvanic state and still maintain a body in physical form. In some cases, they cast off the physical form, electing to remain in a state of bliss in the haven of nirvana.

"I would like to point out here that there are in the land of India and other parts of the world a few unascended beings who have attained such a degree of mastery over form and substance as to remain in one body temple for thousands of years. Some of these are not expected to relinquish their forms until the last individual upon earth has attained his God-victory.

"Such as these have even forsworn the bliss and peace of nirvana in order to serve the holy causes of freedom. They remain alternately in samadhic states or states of bliss and in periods of contact with mankind whereby they bring about wondrous blessings, conferred upon both nations and individuals by their service to life and their very presence upon earth.

"Contrasted to the aforementioned practices and teachings is the goal of the ascension. As we have seen, the ascension has a different connotation than (1) the state of nirvana, or (2) the state of samadhi that is attained through the techniques of yoga, or (3) the state of mastership whereby the holy light of God is conferred upon embodied man in such a manner as to make him almost immortalized in form."[15]

The Highest and Most Revered Guru: The I AM Presence, One with the Christ Self

All Masters, teachers and experiences are meant to lead the individual to the feet of his own guru. But one ought to be careful in accepting the claims of self-styled masters. For unless there is absolute certainty about the qualifications of the teacher, there is always the possibility that such a one will unwittingly misguide his pupils. The safest route to finding God is through attunement with one's own Divine Presence, which hovers ever near the aspiring soul as depicted in the Chart of Your Divine Self (see facing page 74 and pages 244–45).

Through the crystal cord, the lifestream—the energy pulsating from one's own individualized God Presence, I AM—descends into the domain of the Christ Self of each individual, where this great mediator translates the requirements of each hour into straight knowledge. Thus, divine instruction can be conveyed personally to each aspirant through his own Christ Self.

Sometimes those who attach themselves to unascended masters tend to idolize their gurus. But often the chelas are not able to sustain their own exalted opinions of them. Then too, the dark forces of the planet are always looking to destroy men's faith in one another. These do not hesitate to use gossip, circumstantial evidence, and the students' own momentums of fear and doubt to tear down the idol they have fashioned. And so, because the image was not the One Most Holy but an idol to adorn the egos of its makers, it is easily dashed to the ground.

Sometimes the unknowing chela places the idol of the guru so far above himself that it becomes absolutely necessary for him to topple the image in order to regain a sense of his own personal worth and independence. If he only knew that a truly spiritual leader teaches by example, always sees the Christ in his pupils, and never attempts to dominate their lives or their beliefs, he would not feel the need to become involved in this seesaw consciousness.

Wise is the devotee who will guard himself from extremes of thought and feeling. Let him hold to the immaculate concept for all. Then he will not so easily be taken from the light by the dark arrows of destruction that will surely be sent his way, nor will he become a disillusioned victim just when he is beginning to gather greater light into his being.

Long ago, the prophet Jeremiah foretold that the LORD would make a new covenant with the house of Israel: "I will put my law in their inward parts, and write it in their hearts; and will be their God, and they shall be my people. And they shall teach no more every man his neighbor, and every man his brother, saying, Know the LORD: for they shall all know me, from the least of them unto the greatest."[16]

Isaiah also saw that the time would come when "thy teachers [shall not] be removed into a corner any more, but thine eyes shall see thy teachers: And thine ears shall hear a word behind thee, saying, This is the way, walk ye in it."[17] In fulfillment of these inspired sayings, the sure word of prophecy comes to each individual from his God Presence through the mediation of his Christ Self. And this Word that framed the universe will illumine all who will heed the call from on high.

Guides along the Homeward Path

The primary function of the ascended and unascended masters is to help each man to unfold his own latent divinity— but never to do it for him. Their purpose is to help the soul to reestablish her communion with God; with her own threefold flame; with life, Truth and love.

In the service of the light that is the life of men, the masters ascended and unascended bring to the evolutions of this planet illumination, clarification of the laws of God, and verification of ancient knowledge that has been handed down from generation to generation (yet not always in its original form). The courageous stand that they have taken in defense of Truth (even to the point of death) has enabled the many who have followed in their footsteps to be conquerors, both in the world and of the world.

There is neither desecration nor delay in the initiatic process whereby the more highly evolved consciousness imparts to the lesser evolved consciousness a portion of itself. For in the final analysis, the identity of the master under whom one serves and takes his training is not as important as the fact that one has become God-identified and Christ-centered in one's own individual manifestation of the divine consciousness.

And regardless of who the guru may be, it is always the God Presence and the Christ Self of the chela who, through the guru, imparts the gnosis of spiritual wisdom once the chela has committed his being to the disciplines of hierarchy.

The one God and Father of all employs his many manifestations to lead his children along the way that reaches up to him. Sometimes seekers are fooled by the erroneous concept that they have no need of a teacher, either ascended or unascended. They are led to believe by spirits of seduction that they can and should go directly to God and his Christ.

There is nothing wrong with this idea if one can make it work—but to bypass the experience of the Ascended Masters, who know every step of the way, is like setting out upon a jungle expedition without the help of native guides. To ignore the disciplines of the Brotherhood simply to assert one's independence—or even out of a sense of misguided loyalty to God—is wrong. For God himself glories in those servant Sons and Daughters of his heart, who serve only that they may express their love for him.

To deprive men of the blessing of giving themselves in service to less evolved souls or to refuse to receive the ministrations of ascended and ascending beings is to deny the giving of self in service to life. This is the road that leads to nihilism, for one cannot deny another without ultimately denying oneself.

The truly wise and humble are always receptive to those who are well qualified in their field of specialization and to those in the educational systems of the world who can capably direct and encourage their students. In fact, corroboration among scholars and scientists is a means of avoiding repetitious error and unnecessary research. And this applies to the spiritual path as well.

Only by accepting the findings of their predecessors can those who pick up the torch of knowledge advance a particular branch of learning in one brief lifetime. Often these return to continue their investigations right where they left off in a former embodiment.

Wouldn't it be an unfortunate turn of events if these men of discovery were to reject the platform of knowledge that they themselves had served to build, simply because they subsequently refused to come under the tutelage of the acknowledged heads of their specialized fields?

Therefore, are spiritual climbers not wise to refresh themselves on their journey by tarrying at the feet of the Masters?

Among the solitary climbers upon the mountain, there have been a few who have made it alone. But the many have been broken upon the rocks of limited personal experience, and they have suffered setback after setback. If these solitary climbers would leave the peaks of pride and associate with the groups that the hierarchy has established, receiving their instructions from the Ascended Masters or even a true unascended master, they would more quickly and more safely find their way back to the Father's house.

Men must exercise care in their selection of companions on

the Path, lest they become enmeshed in the trivia of the plains. And on the other hand, they might well become the instrument that will draw the souls of fellow seekers into the foothills leading to the summits of self-mastery.

Contamination works both ways, and the true disciples who will follow the Christ are not afraid to move among "sinners" in order that they might infect them with righteousness. As James says, "The wisdom that is from above is first pure, then peaceable, gentle, and easy to be intreated, full of mercy and good fruits, without partiality, and without hypocrisy." Students of the light are needed to raise those who have lost their way. For "unto them that are defiled and unbelieving is nothing pure; but even their mind and conscience is defiled."[18]

Let it be clear that, since Ascended Masters have become wholly one with God through the ritual of the ascension, there is and can be absolutely no competition between them. No struggle on the part of one Master to subvert the students of another is conceivable. Neither would the Ascended Masters at any time feel disrespect for one another.

Those who pay allegiance to only one Ascended Master and fail to acknowledge the panoply of Ascended Beings who represent the consciousness of God in its many jewel-like facets are only cutting themselves off from the universal magnification of the body of God that fulfills the promise of Jesus: "Verily, verily, I say unto you, He that believeth on me, the works that I do shall he do also; and greater works than these shall he do; because I go unto my Father."[19]

Embrace the Entire Spirit of the Great White Brotherhood

Each lifestream who wins his victory embellishes the entire universe. By cutting oneself off from any one of the Ascended

Masters or by speaking disparagingly of him, an individual denies to himself the blessing of the Master's personal momentum of God-victory in his own world.

Universality is all-inclusive. The harmony of all the Masters of Wisdom, both ascended and unascended, is beautiful to behold. This harmony is a symphony of unity that comprises the total outreach upon this planet of the representatives of God who make up the entire Spirit of the Great White Brotherhood.

The existence of these Sons and Daughters of God can never be refuted by human logic. Those who deny the plan of God only deny themselves and their own opportunity to become illustrious servant Sons and Daughters. As the rays of the sun mellow the essence of the solar fires that would consume mere mortals, so do the Sons and Daughters of God temper the light that no man can touch except he too become that light.

Let all feel free to open the doorway of the heart to the eternal God as he expresses himself in the victorious service to life of every Ascended Master. Fortunate is the man who can open his heart to his own destiny, to his own reality, and learn to abide therein by sitting at the feet of the Ascended Masters.

By using the great flames of freedom, by obeying Cosmic Law and by giving strict attention to the guidance of the Ascended Masters, he will more quickly come under the dominion of his own I AM Presence, his great winged God Self, the magnet of pure love. This love will lift him out of the socket of mortal thought and feeling into the deathless, birthless realms of infinite adoration to the one universal God.

Yet an adoration that is not practical, that does not enhance one's service to one's fellowman, is in no way worthy of one's energy. The energies of God are not only for his exaltation in an individual, but also for the implementation of his most practical cosmic service to life.

By following in the footsteps of the great Masters who have walked the earth bearing the torch of divine illumination, each one can add the momentum of his life's victory to the universe as all move onward in the grand halls of the galaxies toward that perfection which originally came forth as the divine image.

The I AM Presence of each one is the Master Instructor who will show the budding consciousness how to manifest the perfection of his divine identity, just as Jesus did. It is the plan of the Creator that each one shall outpicture within himself all that God is. Thus there is established in the life of every soul that order which is heaven's first law.

The Chart of Your Divine Self

Chapter 3

The Summit Lighthouse

*Ours must be a message of infinite love, and we
must demonstrate that love to the world.*

MARK L. PROPHET

The Summit
Lighthouse

FOR THOUSANDS OF YEARS, humanity has been blessed with countless visitations of highly evolved souls—avatars, Buddhas, Christs and Cosmic Beings. Angels have indeed walked with men. Truly God has sent his Son, his light, his radiance to the earth in every generation. Yet, for the most part, as the apostle John so aptly phrased it, the light has shone in the darkness, and the darkness has comprehended it not.[1]

In this age of self-sufficient technology, orthodox theology, and all-embracing materialism, when the forces of darkness threaten to utterly destroy civilization, God has seen fit once again to send a ray of hope to a darkened world.

In August of 1958, the Darjeeling Council of the Great White Brotherhood endorsed the plan of the Ascended Master El Morya to found The Summit Lighthouse. The Karmic Board granted the necessary dispensation for its formation. That month, the first *Pearl of Wisdom* was published in Washington, D.C.

Master Morya, founder of The Summit Lighthouse, is Lord of the First Ray and Chief of the Darjeeling Council.

Through many embodiments he was a dedicated servant of the light. You can read the story of some of these embodiments in *Lords of the Seven Rays*.[2]

The *Pearls of Wisdom* are weekly releases of Ascended Master instruction and are sponsored by the Darjeeling Council. El Morya says: "Our ideas are born within the flaming heart of Truth itself. Fortunate is every one of you who can share in the glorious karma of producing the perfection that we shall externalize through you—if you care to willingly and lovingly serve this cause, in the name and by the authority of Divine Love itself."[3]

El Morya's Dream

As an Ascended Being, El Morya honors the Christ in all men and invites the Ascended Hosts and the spiritually elect among unascended mankind to attend in their finer bodies his council meetings at the Temple of God's Holy Will in Darjeeling. There, seated at the fireside of their gracious host, they seek to foster God-government, good will and universal brotherhood among mankind.

After centuries of service to the will of God, Master Morya saw what great spiritual power could be utilized for the salvation of the planet if all of mankind's energies were focused in the worship of the one God. And he nurtured a dream in his heart. That dream was to gather people from many spiritual endeavors and to offer them the opportunity, through a higher understanding of Cosmic Law, to channel their own Christ light into one great fountain of spiritual effusion—a lighthouse whose powerful beams would sweep over the dark sea of humanity as a beacon of eternal hope.

El Morya envisioned a unity that would replace duality. He saw how the transcendent understanding of the one LORD who is all love would be spread throughout the earth until the golden age would blossom with God-happiness and the Ascended Ones would walk and talk with men as in ages gone by. He founded The Summit Lighthouse as a means for the fulfillment of this dream.

The Master Contacts His Messengers

When the Master contacted us, we offered ourselves to the service of God, conscious that we would fulfill his work "not by might, nor by power, but by my spirit, saith the LORD of hosts."[4] We wanted him to use us to lift the burden of the world, to foster understanding between peoples, to spread the illumination of Truth, and to educate mankind in the mysteries of the Great Law.

Both of us had been under the tutelage of Master Morya since childhood, but it was Mark who established the Summit in 1958. I [Elizabeth] was called in 1961 to assist the expansion of the activity as co-Messenger. El Morya said that our service would involve a lifetime of associated endeavor, and therefore we were married with his blessing in 1963.

When The Summit Lighthouse was incorporated later that year, the Master named Mark as chairman of the board and me as president. He vested us with his authority as twin flames, so that the fullness of his plan might manifest in the balanced action of the masculine and feminine rays.

Although we recognized the achievements of the established religions and their contributions to civilization, we also realized the limitations inherent in the existing structures. We appreciated all of God's revelation to man, but we realized that his revelation must of necessity be progressive.

We saw the workings of Divine Law in the churches, yet we also perceived therein blocks to free thought. We realized that the Masters' teachings could not be disseminated through existing channels. For to some, the Masters' work poses a threat to established dogma. Instead of longing for new insight from the throne of God, they proceed with fear and trembling to defend the bastions of their faith, which have now become prison walls.

As we discussed this "closed-door policy" with the Masters, we were reminded of the words spoken by the Pilgrim minister John Robinson before the Pilgrims embarked on that memorable journey to the New World: "The Lord hath more truth and light yet to break forth out of His holy Word.... If God shall reveal anything to you by any other Instrument of his, be as ready to receive it as ever you were to receive any truth by my Ministry."[5]

Fostering Spiritual Understanding

Archangel Jophiel later explained the founding of The Summit Lighthouse from the standpoint of the evolution of spiritual understanding on the planet:

"The great cosmic reality of the wisdom teachers is not yet in full bloom before the eyes of mankind, because there are many people on this planetary body who have never even heard of the Ascended Master Jesus Christ.... How then can men who are concerned with the link to cosmic hierarchy expect for one moment that mankind who know not the reality of Jesus Christ will know about the Archangels, or about the angelic hosts, or about the Ascended Masters? Today, only relatively few in America are able to create a composite picture of the hierarchy of light.

"When Madame Helena Petrovna Blavatsky in 1875 revealed the Ascended Masters of Wisdom through the Theosophical Society, it was a nova bursting upon the metaphysical sky.... The Ascended Masters continued to work and to pour out into the world an increasing measure of techniques and teachings blessed by the hierarchy of light, while other information was released by the brothers of the shadow to pull men away from the great Mother-lodestone of the infinite Divinity manifest in the Divine Theosophia....

"The Ascended Masters have found it expedient through the years to create new activities of light and to endow them with specific functions in the name of holy progress. I shall explain:

"On the planetary body, individuals of a very devout nature, when they become attached to a specific segment of holy instruction from on high, are often concerned with the enormous responsibility involved in keeping pure the teachings that are vouchsafed to them. Therefore, in their desire to keep the teachings pure, they deny to their followers the right to alter or to change the power structure, the revelatory structure and the messianic message in any way from the state in which it was originally given.

"The Brothers of Wisdom are of the opinion that there is much wisdom in this action. However, because of the rigid stand that is taken by the followers of a specific movement, from time to time it becomes expedient, in order to break the old matrices of thought and feeling, that a new activity of light should be launched.

"Thus the Ascended Masters may take by the hand and head those avant-garde individuals who are willing to be God-taught in every age, who are willing to behold the great onrush of cosmic reality as it parades itself across the sky of their minds, infusing them with ever-new flashes of intuitive intelligence and teaching them techniques destined in the future to give to the children of the coming race a new glimpse of divine reality.

"This then is the reason that The Summit Lighthouse was

endowed by the cosmic hierarchy with the right to function, ordained by God—so that the two Messengers would go forth and proclaim to the world (because of their previous training in connection with the great temple at Tell el-Amarna) the manifestation of the monotheistic technique of the Ascended Masters under the rule of the cosmic panoply or hierarchy of Masters, teaching both the law of the One and the law of the many."

We Stand for Truth

We wish to make clear that The Summit Lighthouse is by no means a by-product of nor a protest movement with respect to any previous religious organization. If its teachings are similar to those of other groups, it is only because both reflect Truth. The Summit Lighthouse stands upon the Truth that has been revealed through prophets and teachers of all ages.

We follow the saints and sages of all religions insofar as they themselves embrace Truth. There is, then, no outer connection between The Summit Lighthouse and any other movement or organization. But there is a definite inner connection between The Summit Lighthouse and the age-old activities of the Great White Brotherhood.

Many have asked whether The Summit Lighthouse is Christian. It is Christian in the truest sense of the word, for our Christianity is founded on the rock of ages, the Christ who overcame the world and who "shall so come in like manner as ye have seen him go."[6] It is founded on the original teachings of Jesus, not on the narrow dogma that men have made of them.

Just as The Summit Lighthouse is broad in its acceptance of Truth as revealed through prophets in all religions, and just as it is tolerant in its outreach to all of God's children upon earth, so it is narrow in its adherence to the spectrum of pure

Truth that unfolds the laws of God.

Jesus said, "Strait is the gate, and narrow is the way, which leadeth unto life."[7] We are willing to follow the lonely road that departs the highway of well-traveled religious thought and leads to the spiritual heights of Christ-regeneration.

The Summit Lighthouse is destined to be a beacon in the history of the evolution of man's religious thinking. It is dedicated to expanding the light of God among mankind as Truth without compromise. Jesus said, "Ye are the light of the world. A city that is set on an hill cannot be hid."[8]

Firmly established upon the rock of the Christ, the Lighthouse beams to the stormy sea of human struggle the message "Peace, be still."[9] The light from the tower is a beacon of hope to a troubled world that yet looks without for a luminary in the social or intellectual sky. It is the light of the Christ that says, "The light that ye seek is ever the light that is in thee."

The standard of Truth must be upheld, and the true teachings of the Christ must be proclaimed. Only the whole Truth will set men free. Therefore we strive to uphold the standard of excellence, to be The Summit Lighthouse, to lead every man into communion with his own Christ Self.

Only then can he become a lighthouse himself—a veritable house of light. Only then can he find the summit of his own being—the Presence of God within him. The God Presence in man is a tower of strength, a pillar in the temple of being. His Causal Body is a guiding light for everyone who would follow the star to the place where the Christ is cradled in his own conscious individuality.

> Let us then be up and doing,
> Holding consort with the few.
> By election, now we're viewing
> All that God was wont to do.

By his light our souls are nourished;
Our delight is in his Law.
Let his kingdom, then, now flourish—
Fill the hearts of men with awe.

Reverence, love and honor shew forth—
We will do it, in God's name.
By the fire of heaven's Spirit
Let us all now keep his flame.

Hold it high, aloft to vision;
Let all see and know precision.
Capture, then, his plan for fusion—
'Tis the end of all confusion.

By the light of oneness showing,
Winds of delusion long now blowing
Will be stilled by light now showing
All the way—O peace, be still.

Take him by the hand and hold it;
Ne'er let go, our Father dear,
Thy great love within us glowing—
Perfect love casts out all fear.

Rectify and purify the world of men;
By the flame of Truth impart
Perseverance from beginning—
Start it now within each heart.

Move it forward by thy power,
Let its light forever shine;
Beam it forth, reveal the flower*
Heaven-sent by hand divine.

---

*The threefold flame.

Christ is Lord—in all he reigneth.
Love enshrines and in all frameth
Script of love that each one claimeth—
Come, dear Lord, and in me reign.

I AM life in all I move,
I AM life to all I prove,
I AM law within thyself,
I AM love's true cosmic wealth.

For everywhere I AM, O thou art,
Everywhere thou art, I AM.
In the beginning and the middle
And at end, I AM, I AM.

Amen.

Goals of The Summit Lighthouse

The goals that the Ascended Masters have proposed for The Summit Lighthouse are many. These include the preparation of the Christ children, the Buddhas, and the incoming avatars for their mission and for the initiations leading to their ascension, as well as the preparation of all who are willing to undergo the rigors of initiation prescribed by the hierarchy for acceptance into the Ascension Temple—either at the close of this embodiment or while the body sleeps.

Through the teachings of the Ascended Masters published by The Summit Lighthouse, the requirements for the ascension are made so plain that the Queen of Light's prophecy of mass ascensions on the hillsides[10] will one day become a reality.

Educational programs must be established for all age levels from preschool to the university level—where young people will be taught about the Christ and his teachings on Cosmic Law and parents will be taught to nurture the Christ in their children and in themselves.

We must sponsor the music of the spheres, which carries the matrix for the golden age. We must train parents and teachers who will sponsor the seventh root race, and we must preserve the link with hierarchy for coming generations. The Summit must leave a written record for those who have not been quickened by the Spirit, that they might find Truth in future embodiments.

Finally, the foundation must be laid for the golden age, setting forth the teachings of the Brotherhood and writing the sacred scriptures for the next two-thousand-year cycle. We must write the Everlasting Gospel of God, of which these volumes are the first chapter.

The Summit promotes self-purification, self-mastery, preparation for the ascension, and continual progression into greater light and greater attunement with the Presence. Through this activity, the Masters are constantly engaged in the recovery of the lost Word, in the regeneration of millions of lifestreams, and in the removal of subconscious barriers through the power of the sacred fire.

It is possible to rephrase old truths, cloaking them with the freshness of a new perspective. The Master said that our goals are the salvation of the planet, the freedom of man, and the perpetual joy of God that can be made known to all. He told us that there is a great treasury of wisdom concerning God's infinite laws, which has not yet been released unto mankind.

He also warned that for us to release the superstructure of the building without putting it upon a sound foundation would not be an orderly process. There must be relevance. Therefore we must build upon the foundation of Truth that has already been revealed to the prophets of old, and continue with the knowledge that the Masters would unfold through us.

The Law of the I AM

The Master then proceeded to reveal to us the Law of the I AM. He said that the I AM Law is the highest and oldest law in creation. It was first affirmed in recorded history by Moses, who heard God proclaim out of the burning bush, "I AM THAT I AM."[11]

El Morya told us that it is the being of God that constitutes the image of God. Inasmuch as man is made in the divine image, that image is man's sole reality. God is the Word, and the Word is the Christ, and this Word, by whom all things were made, went forth as the power of the I AM who said, "I AM the way, the Truth and the life" and "I AM the resurrection and the life."[12]

The Master also reminded us that the Chart of Your Divine Self (facing page 74) could never be more than a symbol of the infinite Causal Body of man with its concentric spheres of color.

He said that the chart should include a representation of the Christ Self (or Higher Mental Body) because man now lives in a time when the second coming of Christ may be seen as the Lord coming suddenly into his temple with the rush of a mighty wind. God will claim the temple of man's being as the power of the Higher Mental Body and the Paraclete (or Holy Spirit) enters the chalice, the body and being of man.

Because the dark and divisive forces work continually against the law of the One (the law of man's being and his link with eternity), many attempts have been made to discredit those who in every age have stood for the principle of the I AM.

Inasmuch as "I AM" is the name of God, every man,

woman, and child upon earth has the right to rejoice in it, to
live in it, and to change the world by it until the world reflects
the splendor that is already within the Mind of God—as
Above, so below.

The Summit as an Avenue of the Great White Brotherhood

Master El Morya said: "Those who know the meaning of
real love understand that the Great White Brotherhood has
many avenues through which to express its many beautiful
activities, and refuses in the holy name of freedom and liberty
to be limited in its approach to planetary assistance by mere
human ideas of the self-styled elect!"

He continued: "As I have intimated before, the Brotherhood has only within the past few months and years begun to
externalize through The Summit Lighthouse some of our most
hopeful ideas and plans for humanity. Our great hope is to
create a haven of such light that no human quality can ever
enter in or abide.

"Wise men will understand its 'live and let live' policy as
being of our making. They will not foolishly deem its attitude
Pollyannaish or weak, seeing rather that in unity with God,
Truth and the Ascended Masters' way there is strength victori-
ous! As a potent, expanding facet of the Brotherhood, The
Summit Lighthouse is one of our greatest avenues."[13]

Later El Morya expanded on this point: "Understandable
is it that each organization demands some form of loyalty of its
adherents, but unfortunately 'all or nothing at all' seems to be
the requirement of many religious orders. Only your I AM
Presence has the right to ask all of any part of life.

"Loyalty to Truth, to your friends, and to high standards
or principles is good, but no one should ever permit himself to

be dominated or controlled by any person, place, condition or thing except the Ascended Masters and his own God Presence. Yet, of course, those of like mind should ever be willing to lovingly assist one another in effecting the many aspects of the eternal purposes.

"It does not appear to be clear to many people that the Ascended Masters and the Great White Brotherhood often have ordained or directed individuals in the past—even assisting them in forming an organization or group through which the Masters and the Brotherhood could disseminate information and render a profound service.

"And then they find that at a later date the control of these same groups or organizations was wrested away from the Masters and the Brotherhood, while the activity degenerated into a mere outer husk or shell of its former self. One thing that has made this particularly confusing is the fact that often these religious orders or philosophical groups continue to grow or prosper outwardly, still disseminating many of the truths of the Great Ones."[14]

Lord Lanto, Chohan of the second ray, announced: "Because this activity is builded so solidly upon the rock, I, Lanto, declare in wisdom's name that it shall stand to fulfill El Morya's dream. Those who have aided it shall be so grateful one day that they did, as they see just why Utopia did come into manifestation because of their cooperation, constancy, and determination to *be* Christs in action."[15]

A Weekly Outpouring of Wisdom

Through the *Pearls,* the Masters are making available the wisdom of the ages. Those who receive the *Pearls of Wisdom* are bound by no rules of conduct or statement of faith. They are asked only to assist, if possible, with the nominal publication and mailing costs.

El Morya comments: "Knowing that faith and harmony are ever a part of the light and that The Summit Lighthouse asks no special fealty or allegiance other than your love for deeper contact with us, I trust that all of you who love the Truth of which I speak will continue to enjoy the *Pearls of Wisdom* for a long time to come—until in God's memory-record of light you become illustrious and in manifestation self-luminous.

"Then, as one of us, you will need no other thread of contact, having attained the glory of full reunion that you ever and always seek. The continuing support you give to the physical activity of The Summit Lighthouse in the future will, as it did in the past, make possible my continuing allotment of spiritual energy in the weekly releases of the *Pearls of Wisdom*. You see, we cannot give it all—Cosmic Law decrees that part must come from your side of the veil. Whatever you do, do in good will. For in God one is indeed never alone, but All-One!"[16]

We Seek the Response of Men's Hearts

Of course, students of the Ascended Masters are free to retain membership in the church of their choice. El Morya says:

"Men and women then of every faith or national origin: We appeal to you to see here an opportunity to express the highest tenets of your faith itself—which, if it exists at all, must be within your hearts—and, therefore, the end result of peace and victory that we hope to obtain shall not come about alone because of either personality or organization, but because of the response of men's hearts. Do you see?

"The Summit Lighthouse itself *is* The Summit Lighthouse because it elects to stand for the highest and best in all men, in people of every faith and nation, for the purest victory for the earth and her people. We intend not only the highest and best spiritually for all, but the release through this doorway of the finest and best educational material for all, which will help men to live in happiness and harmony forevermore."[17]

He also tells us: "There is an ever-increasing need for expansion of the Ascended Masters' teaching in opposition to all anti-Christ distortions and errors. It was with this end in view that we secured the permission of Helios and Vesta and the Great Karmic Board to originally create The Summit Lighthouse.

"This was not to absorb religions or ideologies, but rather to serve as a cosmic springboard where the forte of Truth would be expanded and expounded our way, free from commercialization or exploitation by the ego. Thus many thirsty travelers would find such refreshment of the Spirit in godly simplicity that a general expansion of divine world good would ensue quite naturally!"[18]

Lanto has expressed the concern of the Brotherhood over the fact that there is little they can do in times of world crisis because the Masters can answer only when called upon. He says:

"The key to it all lies in the expansion in the world of form of knowledge about the Brothers of Light, about the spiritual hierarchy, about the Ascended Masters, about the natural unfoldment of the individual through his own I AM Presence.

"Unless this be done, the world will not suddenly turn to the light. It has never been enough simply to produce great lights in the world. Some of these go down in the halls of fame and are remembered in the annals of every age. But deeds are more important than names, and the face of pure Truth is more important than to speak about it."[19]

We conclude with Henry Wadsworth Longfellow's poem

"The Lighthouse," which is too prophetic to be omitted from this chapter on the Summit.

The Lighthouse

The rocky ledge runs far into the sea,
    And on its outer point, some miles away,
The Lighthouse lifts its massive masonry,
    A pillar of fire by night, of cloud by day.

Even at this distance I can see the tides,
    Upheaving, break unheard along its base,
A speechless wrath, that rises and subsides
    In the white lip and tremor of the face.

And as the evening darkens, lo! how bright,
    Through the deep purple of the twilight air,
Beams forth the sudden radiance of its light
    With strange, unearthly splendor in the glare!

Not one alone; from each projecting cape
    And perilous reef along the ocean's verge,
Starts into life a dim, gigantic shape,
    Holding its lantern o'er the restless surge.

Like the great giant Christopher it stands
    Upon the brink of the tempestuous wave,
Wading far out among the rocks and sands,
    The night o'ertaken mariner to save.

And the great ships sail outward and return,
    Bending and bowing o'er the billowy swells,
And ever joyful, as they see it burn,
    They wave their silent welcomes and farewells.

They come forth from the darkness, and their sails
   Gleam for a moment only in the blaze,
And eager faces, as the light unveils,
   Gaze at the tower, and vanish while they gaze.

The mariner remembers when a child,
   On his first voyage, he saw it fade and sink,
And when, returning from adventures wild,
   He saw it rise again o'er ocean's brink.

Steadfast, serene, immovable, the same
   Year after year, through all the silent night
Burns on forevermore that quenchless flame,
   Shines on that inextinguishable light!

It sees the ocean to its bosom clasp
   The rocks and sea-sand with the kiss of peace;
It sees the wild winds lift it in their grasp,
   And hold it up, and shake it like a fleece.

The startled waves leap over it; the storm
   Smites it with all the scourges of the rain,
And steadily against its solid form
   Press the great shoulders of the hurricane.

The sea-bird wheeling round it, with the din
   Of wings and winds and solitary cries,
Blinded and maddened by the light within,
   Dashes himself against the glare, and dies.

A new Prometheus, chained upon the rock,
   Still grasping in his hand the fire of Jove,
It does not hear the cry, nor heed the shock,
   But hails the mariner with words of love.

"Sail on!" it says, "sail on, ye stately ships!
    And with your floating bridge the ocean span;
Be mine to guard this light from all eclipse,
    Be yours to bring man nearer unto man!"

Chapter 4

The Messengers

Remember the Messenger and the Sender, even as you forget not the message or the sending.... The coming of the Messenger is always the preparing of the way for the coming of a new level of the Christ consciousness.

EL MORYA

The Messengers

THE TRUE PROPHET OF GOD is the Messenger of God. God speaks through Messengers today just as he spoke through the prophets of the Old Testament. Indeed, every age needs a Messenger from God, for in every age the Ascended Masters are permitted by Cosmic Law to release greater teachings on the Law. They are permitted to reveal the precepts that will enable mankind to disentangle themselves from the web of karma and from the forces that use that karma against them.

The Ascended Master Lanto says, "Without cosmic revelation all men would be ultimately dead." In other words, without the contact with the Most High that provides man with a greater purpose than a merry-go-round whirl for threescore years and ten, "life is but an empty dream"[1] where man walks among the dead and knows not that he too is spiritually dead.

There is no such thing as final revelation, for revelation is ever coming forth from the I AM Presence and Christ Self of every individual as the still, small voice within. It is also coming forth through lifestreams God ordains to serve as lightbearers to focus his wisdom and to make it practical for the age.

Beloved Kuthumi points out: "When we pause to consider the wealth of Ascended Master instruction that has been given in the past as avant-garde spiritual information, we perceive that one of the reasons so much of it has not been appropriated is that some have limited our release of spiritual information according to certain misinterpretations of Cosmic Law taken from the sacred scriptures of the world.

"For example, the admonishment 'Ye shall not add unto the word which I command you, neither shall ye diminish aught from it'[2] certainly was not intended to forestall the privilege of the eternal Father to release from the treasure-house of his being, through his emissaries and teachers, through his prophets and revelators, transcendent information for each advancing age.

"To diminish or to take away from the Word is to delete from consciousness the eternal truths, the timeless truths of God, by failing to recognize the divine intent hidden within the Word. The adding to the Word of extraneous matter is the adding of distortion from the levels of the human intellect to the pure teachings of the Universal Christ, which are the same yesterday, today and forever.[3]

"On the other hand, the statement of the angel who released the Book of Revelation to John the Beloved 'Seal not the sayings of the prophecy of this book'[4] signifies that Revelation is an open book, to be continued by God's appointed representatives for the enlightenment of every age.

"Transcendence is progressive change, and the nature of God with all of its absolute beauty becomes more magnificent each moment. If it were not so, the advancing souls of the Ascended Beings would come to a point in the Absolute where all things would be attained and they would no longer experience that holy anticipation—that joyous expectancy for the cornucopia of progress and expanding awareness—that is so much a part of the unfoldment of the Divine in man at every stage of his development.

"It is, then, the nature of God to increase the vibratory action of the Godhead itself, so that all of creation can always move progressively in the direction of greater happiness, greater achievement and greater wisdom."[5]

The Messenger of God Within

Every man has his own messenger in the person of his own Christ Self. Without contact with the mediator of the Christ Self, man loses contact with his own God Presence. In the first three golden ages, before the descent of mankind's consciousness into the dense spheres of duality, the sons and daughters of God relied upon the Christ within to teach them the knowledge of the Law, while the Manus set the example for the Christ-pattern they were to outpicture.

The hierarchical office of Messenger was therefore not established until mankind lost contact with the inner voice and were no longer able to hear the Word of the Lord or to receive directly the instruction of the Ascended Masters. God provided the missing link to hierarchy in the ages of darkness when mankind knew not the way in which they should go.

At present, the Messengers are serving to reestablish each man's contact with his own Christ Self. Through the instruction on the Law that the Ascended Masters are delivering, every man in Christ will one day be able to discern what is Truth. He will know the difference between the "mutterings and peepings" of familiar spirits and the voice of God himself.

Isaiah prophesied that the time would come when the "teachers" (the Christ Selves) would not be removed into a corner anymore, when "thine eyes shall see thy teachers: And thine ears shall hear a word behind thee, saying, This is the way, walk ye in it, when ye turn to the right hand, and when ye turn to the left."[6]

Until the time comes when each man shall sit under his own vine and fig tree[7] (his own crystal cord and I AM Presence), there will be a need for Messengers.

The Functions of God's Messengers

The primary function of a Messenger is to act as a sensor of the Ascended Master's Presence, attuning with the Master and acting as his hands, his feet, his mouth and his direct representative in the world of form.

While Messengers or prophets of God have not always manifested the fullness of Christ-perfection in their outer consciousness but have on occasion exhibited human traits, their purified consciousness—their dedication to God and to the Masters— is complete within itself. They have always sought to transcend their limitations and to increase their spiritual attainment.

The office of Messenger is carried out from the level of the Christ Self. In other words, when a Messenger is acting as the mouthpiece of God, the instruction comes forth from the level of his own Christ Self as an expression of the Christ Selves of all mankind, as admonishment to those who are in a state of becoming the Christ but who as yet do not hear the voice of their Lord. Therefore, such communication will not be in conflict with private revelation if the latter is accurate.

Neither does the service of one Messenger ever preclude the good that has been done by those who have gone before, for all Messengers of God are one. Their office in hierarchy is under the World Teachers, who in turn serve under the Lord of the World and the Great Central Sun Messengers.

True prophets of God and Messengers of the Great White Brotherhood have progressively attained to a higher degree of efficiency in their predictions and activities for the hierarchy. Several thousand years ago, the biblical prophets were considered to be from 50 to 65 percent accurate. Early in this century, the prophets were considered to be from 90 to 95 percent accurate, and currently the Messengers are considered to be from 95 to 98 percent accurate in their transmittals to mankind. (These percentages were obtained from the Ascended Master Saint Germain.)

The Messenger, then, brings forth through the written and spoken Word the instruction that the invisible Teachers would impart to their unascended disciples.

In all cases, Messengers are sensitive, reliable lifestreams who have proven their worthiness to serve the hierarchy through many embodiments. Their attunement with the hierarchy and the God Presence, together with the preparation they have made at inner levels, enables them to act as mediators between the higher realms of light and the four lower levels of earthly consciousness.

Beloved Morya says: "These gifted and cosmically ordained prophets are God's telephone, a divine instrument through which the Masters of light may speak without human interference."[8]

The ritual of ordaining a Messenger, which is conducted by a member of the hierarchy, takes place only after years of intensive preparation, both during the embodiment in which he serves and during countless previous lives that may extend over thousands of years.

The Requirements of the Office of Messenger

Every office in hierarchy has its requirements, and the office of Messenger is no exception. There are certain inner initiations that must be passed. Unless the individual who has been called to that office has surrendered the ego and the human will to the Divine Ego and the Divine Will, he is considered unfit to hold the office.

In our case, it was the Ascended Master El Morya who trained our lifestreams for this service in this embodiment. He organized a program of initiation and study especially suited to each of our lifestreams.

Mark served beloved K-17 for many years before he took public dictations from members of the hierarchy. Although he held and still holds other offices in the Brotherhood, the formal dedication of his lifestream and the ceremony of his ordination took place shortly before the formation of The Summit Lighthouse in 1958.

The training that I [Elizabeth] had been given at inner levels and in previous embodiments continued through my childhood. The ceremony of my ordination was conducted in 1963 by the Ascended Master Saint Germain in the presence of twelve witnesses in Washington, D.C.

The Messenger's Contact with the Brotherhood

He who holds the office of Messenger receives certain cosmic keys that the Masters anchor in his four lower bodies, as well as the sacred science and technique of contact with the ascended octaves. Without these keys and the accompanying techniques, no amount of training can give the individual the assurance that he has indeed tuned in to Ascended Master levels of consciousness.

The keys that are anchored in the Messenger's four lower bodies as hieroglyphs of the Spirit—cosmic computers in capsule form—give him instantaneous contact with the Brotherhood at any hour of the day or night.

As the reverse is also true, the Messenger is the Brotherhood's immediate point of contact in times of crisis, catastrophe or great urgency, when those who are part of the mass consciousness are in too great a turmoil to be able to make the necessary attunement with the God Presence.

The Messengers can be depended upon to receive the Word of God that contains within itself the power to still the storm and the raging of human emotion, and to channel into every negative condition the healing unguents of Truth.

The technique of contact (which allows the Messenger to use the keys) includes certain rituals that the Messenger must perform before taking a dictation, one of which is the locking of his mind within the vibratory frequency of the Master who is dictating. This is done by means of what El Morya has called the thread of contact.

Saint Germain says that the thread of contact is usually somewhat gossamer in appearance but is actually very strong. Like a diamond cable of light, it can resist the "din of dissonance" (as El Morya often calls the voices of the brothers of shadow) and can conduct the mighty currents of God's glory, bringing blessings to all the world.[9]

How Dictations Are Received

The hierarchy communicates with the Messenger over light and sound rays. Those who have studied the Masters' instruction and those who have seen and heard dictations may be interested to know that messages are received in several ways:

1. In letters of living fire that appear before the Messenger, who reads them as one would read the letters that appear on a moving marquee. Invisible to the audience, these letters move across the screen of the Messenger's mind as if they were on a conveyer belt.

2. Ex cathedra, from the mouth of God, when the Ascended

Master superimposes his Electronic Presence over the Messenger, making his voice box congruent with the Messenger's and using it as if it were his own. In this case the transfer of thought from the Master's consciousness to the Messenger's is instantaneous, and there is no intermediate process whereby the Messenger must discern or read the words. This form of dictation comes through with great rapidity and is usually flawless.

3. Through thoughtforms released by the Master from his consciousness to the Messenger's. These are capsules that contain the matrices for the dictation. They are decoded in the Messenger's brain through a computerized process. By means of the keys that have been inserted into his four lower bodies, the patterns of the Master are translated to the Messenger's wavelength and then are formulated into words.

This is a complicated process that takes place independently of the time-space continuum. The Mind of Christ, superimposed as a halo over the Messenger, is congruent with the Mind of God individualized in the Ascended Master.

4. Direct telepathy used by the Master to release mental patterns to the Messenger through the Mind of Christ. This form of dictation is used when the Master is not present but is in his retreat or at another point in this solar system. This method is also used for brief comments that the Messenger may solicit from the Master on organizational matters or as personal counseling for students.

5. Over the thread of contact that connects the Messenger with the entire Spirit of the Great White Brotherhood simultaneously. As he is connected with each individual member of the Brotherhood, the Messenger can receive telepathically such information as the Masters deem vital to his service in the world of form.

Each method of receiving dictations serves a different purpose. The ex cathedra method is the highest and best form, for it enables the Master to extend his aura with greater intensity into the atmosphere of the room and into the auras of those who are physically present. Thus they are able to take in with all of their faculties the Master's message, as well as the release of his radiation.

However, when there are disturbing elements in the room such as those who are skeptical of or out of harmony with the Masters, the Messengers or their teachings, it is possible for them to interfere with the transmission of the ex cathedra dictation to such an extent that the Master finds it expedient to relay the message either telepathically or in letters of fire.

The rapidity of speech and the flow of ideas in the dictations is, in many cases, superhuman. The Messenger has no idea what the content of the dictation will be prior to the moment that it is received. Moreover, he often does not even know who will be dictating. Therefore, it is preposterous to suppose that the Messenger has premeditated upon either the topic or the sequences of the worded concepts.

It is not even within the capacity of a human being to develop, on the instant, an intelligently organized speech and then to deliver it with the speed with which the dictations come forth. The memorization of such a lengthy discourse would be equally difficult.

The representative of the Holy Spirit says: "I am amazed that mankind can imagine in their own vanities that this Messenger would have the ability to express himself as I do; and I compliment them upon their foolish imaginations.

"Those who think for one moment that this Messenger has the power—although he has some power of speech—to speak as I am speaking, are in effect betraying the energies of heaven. For I assure you that we are endowing him now with our graces, that you may partake of heavenly manna."[10]

The Intuitive Faculties of God's Messengers

Those who are steeped in dogma are not able to discover in the dictations the subtle keys that are often self-evident to more advanced chelas. As one tends to become that to which he is exposed, so the Messenger and the chelas of the Ascended Masters tend to acquire the qualities of the Divine, of an Ascended Being, of an angel, of an Archangel or of a Cosmic Being, when exposed to the vibratory action of their consciousness.

Thus, the intuitive faculties and the abilities of discernment that all Messengers have are by no means unique to them. These can be developed to a greater or lesser degree by any sincere disciple and are, of course, very helpful in corroborating the testimony of the prophets themselves.

Whenever an Ascended Master such as Jesus Christ chooses to dictate a message to the mankind of earth through one of his chosen Messengers, there is an accompanying release of the vibratory action and the high thoughts and energy patterns of the Master himself. Those who are sensitive and are able to feel these vibratory actions are often raised in consciousness far above their ordinary state.

Certainly, those who feel the Master's presence do not question intellectually that which is already confirmed by the heart. They have felt the radiant release that moves in waves through the nerve centers, realigning the thought patterns and producing feeling patterns of wonderful harmony. However, those who have not yet opened their spiritual centers need a great deal of faith in order to assimilate the truth about prophecy.

Do Not Judge the Teaching by the Imperfections of Its Messenger

In reply to students' questions concerning the nature of prophecy, Saint Germain said:

"We have been asked to define prophecy. Those who lack discrimination, torn between the desire to believe all things and plagued by honest doubt, yearn for clarification from heavenly places.

"Remember that all of the sacred books that have ever been written, all of the knowledge that is esteemed by the many religions of the world—regardless of the claims of men to the contrary—have come into manifestation through individuals who were embodied upon the planet. In other words, they have all come forth through man.

"There is and has always been a tendency on the part of mankind to judge the accuracy and quality of spiritual material by the lives of those through whom the material came. We have said that men should not spend as much time as they do in using the mortal mind to examine the lives or persons of spiritual teachers. We have said that thirsty travelers ought not spurn a cup of cold water, simply because the tin cup in which it is delivered has an imperfection in it.

"If the world is old, every individual on earth is old—in the sense that myriad experiences have created encrusted concepts that are difficult for men to relinquish. Thus as in olden times even to the present hour, men do examine the source of information rather than the teaching. And it is the teaching, after all, that is everything.

"That which bears the earmark of cosmic authenticity registers within the chords of the heart. But how shall this be manifest in those whose attunement with their own hearts is sadly lacking, where the brittleness of the mind can analyze only the worded structure of our releases?

"Where, then, is the sounding board for authenticity? Men should understand that they themselves need perfectionment as well as attunement with the higher powers, if they are to register the genuine perfection that they profess to seek.

"You see, frequently seekers for light maintain a very unprofessional attitude in their examination of the various teachings they encounter. But after all, they lack experience in that which they seek. Therefore, there is almost a blind struggle that occurs in the world of men on the path toward the light.

"Is it any wonder, then, that they are easily victimized by the blind leaders of the blind who themselves have attained not one iota of God-realization? They study the lives of the saints, yet they permit themselves to hold others in contempt.

"Heaven is not disdainful of honest men's search for Truth, but we know that people are prone to be critical of those whose simplest thoughts they cannot understand. Human sophistry and wit do not of themselves lead to higher dimensions and accurate perceptions.

"On the contrary, many have excommunicated themselves from a movement of definite spiritual progress before they could take root or refuge in an onward-moving company of spiritual devotees. Surely this must pinpoint for the perceptive how very vital it is that men be as little children, trusting in the Infinite One and in the wisdom of heaven itself to perform judgment upon men whose hypocrisy they eschew.

"There is no need, blessed ones, for men to be constantly engaged in a witch-hunt while they yet seek to find their way back home. Again and again, individuals steeped in tradition or in traditional concepts attend one of our services, only to turn away from the great opportunity that is given to them.

"For ere the door can be opened to the light or valid explanations given, they have already decided that the appearance or speech of those who represent us is not pleasing to them. Arbiters of their own confusion are they, laying hold upon decaying substance and proclaiming it as real, while turning away from the real and the banner of freedom without ever knowing what its true value is.

"I admit that some things are self-evident and cast their shadows before them, but Truth is often subtly concealed beneath a crude exterior or a manifestation that belies its great content. If there is, then, any admonishment that I would give to humanity in these troubled times it is this: Be not hasty of judgment."[11]

Messengers Do Not Engage in Astral or Psychic Practices

There is a big difference between the Messenger who represents the hierarchy by divine appointment and the channel or medium of astral personalities and vibrations. It is impossible for the Messenger of God to be involved in any form of spiritualism, for his consciousness is not at the level of the astral plane where the spirits dwell.

Neither is it possible for him to be involved in trance. There is nothing mediumistic about the work of the true prophets of God. The consciousness of the Messenger must be purified by the Holy Spirit and transformed by the Mind of Christ. Only when functioning from the level of that Spirit and that Mind is he able to contact the ascended consciousness of the Master and thereby bring forth his dictations.

The Brotherhood does not allow the Messenger to engage in trance or automatic writing, nor does it recommend that the true disciple of the Christ engage in these practices. This is simply because when one turns over his consciousness to someone who is not perfected—whose consciousness gravitates to the astral plane—he is subject to that one's *total* consciousness.

Not only do the words and thoughts of the discarnate pass to the channel, but so does his entire momentum—a literal sewer of untransmuted substance. The same is true when the medium is hypnotized. Moreover, even though early in this century the Ascended Masters provided for spirit communication on a limited basis for the purpose of establishing proof of existence beyond the grave, they have withdrawn that dispensation because so many abuses occurred.

Psychic Mediums and Communication with Disembodied Souls

At present, the Brotherhood has an extensive program of instruction in their etheric retreats for souls preparing to reembody. Thus these souls should not remain in the lower strata for such activities as spirit communication. Any indication of the presence of departed loved ones or astral so-called guides should be one's signal to make calls for them to be taken swiftly to octaves of light and the retreats of the Brotherhood.

There is definite karma in magnetizing unascended disembodied souls. These souls should be set free to pursue nobler purposes, while those embodied here below should cleave only to the I AM Presence and the Ascended Hosts of light, whose presence in our midst we are privileged to enjoy.

Where there are true prophets, there are often those who—while they may be sincere—are victims of their own illusions. Their light is stolen through their involvement in the glamour of the psychic realm, and they serve as tools of psychic personalities. They disseminate teachings cloaked in light, whose core is actually misqualified energy or darkness. Their words may appear to convey wisdom, but the effect of their words can be shattering. Indeed, many levels of truth and error are often indiscriminately presented to the unwary.

It is our studied opinion that the majority of mediums are more the victims of their own delusions than they are the willful deceivers of men. This does not lessen the dangers for their followers, but the sincere follower of a false prophet can readily adapt himself to the Truth once he has found it.

Many communications received by mediums are but the thrust of impostors who cleverly cloak their words in a steady practice of deceiving even the mediums through whom they speak. Often it is the entity who intends to deceive mankind, not the medium. And the entity is deceived by the archdeceiver himself, the ally of world negation.

Indeed, the false hierarchy has representatives both in and out of embodiment who imitate the dictations of the Ascended Masters, hoping to preempt the activities of the true hierarchy of light. The false hierarchs send their unwitting tools on supposed errands of the Brotherhood and direct them to establish centers that are purportedly under the sponsorship of the true hierarchy, but are actually outposts of confusion set up to deliberately snare well-meaning seekers and to lure them from the one true Path.

There are two ways in which one can test those who claim to be the representatives of the Brotherhood—by their vibrations and by their teachings. If their vibrations are of darkness, then their teachings will be partially or wholly inaccurate, for they themselves do not have the ability to contact the light while they remain in darkness.

Therefore, that which they bring forth must be based on what the true prophets of God have already brought forth. Dwellers of the night, they are not qualified to be teachers of men, for their vibrations will always taint the teachings as well as the souls to whom they impart them. They will not possess the fire of the Christ that is able by the power of the spoken

Word to quicken the hearts of the many and to draw all men unto him.

On the other hand, if their vibrations are good but their teachings are falsely based, they must be tutored by the Christ in a correct understanding of the laws of God before they go forth to sow bad seed among good and later reap the harvest thereof.

Powers of the Messenger

Although the Messenger has the power to read all levels of human consciousness, including the akashic records, he never does so by the power of the human mind and its involvement with the human side of life, but always through the third eye that is tethered to the I AM Presence, always through the Mind of Christ.

The Messenger has pledged never to use this gift for the entertainment or the flattery of egos, but only at the behest of a member of hierarchy on behalf of an unascended chela.

Among the other powers given to the Messenger are gifts of healing, discerning of spirits, speaking in tongues, and the casting out of demons and discarnate entities. The Messenger retains these gifts only as long as he uses them for the specific purposes outlined by the hierarchy, for the blessing of human-ity, and for purposes in accordance with the law of karma and Cosmic Law.

The Messenger, the true prophet, has a calling from God. That calling was given to him when the Almighty fashioned the archetypal pattern for the destiny of twin flames. "And how shall they preach, except they be sent? as it is written, How beautiful are the feet of them that preach the gospel of peace, and bring glad tidings of good things!"[12]

We Come in the Name of a Prophet

We come, then, to the subject of our own Messengership. Because some have thought that our surname was selected for business purposes, we wish to say that it was given to Mark L. Prophet by his earthly parents, Thomas and Mabel Prophet. It was a divine bequest for which we are grateful.

We have been asked whether we were chosen because of the purity of our being or our high state of spiritual progress. We have been asked whether we are unascended masters, saints or exalted beings.

To these questions we reply: If there be any virtue, if there be any light, if there be any blessings coming forth to the followers of the Christ in the place where we stand, let men look up and acknowledge the Source of all Good. For we are only servants of God, by no means perfected, only willing to raise the chalice of our consciousness that all might drink of the living water of eternal Truth.[13]

Often we are so humbled by the great height from which the divine energies are released that we cry, "Lord, I am not worthy," and to this he replies, "The Christ in every man is worthy to receive me; so are ye also worthy."

Sanat Kumara, First Messenger and Keeper of the Flame

Students of the occult often inquire about our past embodiments. Quite understandably, they wish to know our "credentials." Although we look to the God within every man and to his present realization of that God, we also realize that a man's past performances set the sail of his soul in future lives. Therefore, to satisfy the questions of would-be adherents of Ascended Master Law, we offer the following information concerning our inheritance from the past.

Our service to the evolutions of this planet began with the advent of Sanat Kumara (the Ancient of Days), who came from Venus to keep the flame of the Christ blazing for the mankind of earth at the time of the planet's greatest crisis. The earth had already been besieged by the laggards and the Luciferian hordes, and under their influence her evolutions had been reduced to the level of cavemen.

The earth provided a great challenge to unascended souls evolving on other planetary homes in this system. Its evolutions no longer emitted light, for all had forgotten their Source. The earth stood at the point of being dissolved by cosmic decree.

The evolutions of sister planets, remembering the fate of the destroyed planet Maldek (whose remains still circle the sun as the asteroid belt between Mars and Jupiter), appealed to Solar Lords for intercession on the earth's behalf.

Sanat Kumara, hierarch of Venus, went before the cosmic councils, volunteering to leave his home and consort to keep the flame for the evolutions of earth who had been led astray through outside interference. He was the first Messenger to the planet and the first Keeper of the Flame. Realizing his great courage, many volunteered to accompany him.

These volunteers came not only from Venus but also from other planets and stars beyond our solar system. They knew that once they embodied, the chances were very great that they would become involved in karma-making situations that would tie them to their adopted home for perhaps thousands of years. Nevertheless, they had been trained to render this service, and the opportunity beckoned.

For many centuries, the thousands of lifestreams composing the retinue of Sanat Kumara remained in his service at etheric levels at Shamballa, the retreat of the Lord of the World situated over the Gobi Desert. But there came a time when through their ministration from etheric levels the general consciousness of the race was raised to such a level that Sanat Kumara considered it safe for the volunteers to embody.

Under his direction, they were commissioned to go forth into the world of form to carry his light. Two by two they took embodiment, until an entire wave of Venusian and other interplanetary volunteers were firmly entrenched in the karmic patterns of the earth. Among these were our own twin flames.

Higher Service

It is not unusual for a Messenger to be of the evolutions of another planet. Jesus himself and many of the world's great thinkers and leaders in every field of endeavor have come with the message of the Brotherhood as volunteers from other planets in this solar system and even other systems.

In 1965, Casimir Poseidon announced that we had been offered the guardianship of the Lake Titicaca retreat after its two current hierarchs, the God and Goddess Meru, have been advanced in cosmic service. In preparation for that position in hierarchy, we were given a crown of illumination and were made Prince and Princess of the Holy Order of God and Goddess Meru. We are to be overshadowed by these two great beings of light throughout the remainder of this embodiment in order that we may absorb illumination's ray.[14]

The Messengers Bear the Brunt of Opposition

The Great Divine Director has said:

"Little do you dream of the energies that have attacked these beloved Messengers to prevent the dictations from coming through with smoothness, with clarity and with peace so that their blessed hearts could rejoice in knowing that they had performed most beautifully according to requirements made of their lifestreams.

"Well, precious ones of the light, you must always remember that the prow of a ship must sometimes take a ferocious beating during a storm. Why is this so? Because as it parts the waves it is the instrument that contacts them first.

"You must understand, then, that these Messengers are also instruments through which we contact you. But we contact them first with our energy, and then the energy flows out into your world.

"Quite naturally then, just as an arrowhead that penetrates substance will also receive a great deal more of a blow than the feathers that are at the shaft end of the arrow, you can plainly see that these beloved Messengers will from time to time receive the brunt of a physical attack as well as a psychic attack, mounted against them in order to disturb the equanimity of their beings and thus to prevent the manifestation of the radiance we desire to furnish to every student of the light."[15]

The Messengers at the End of the Age

We conclude this chapter with the interpretation of the eleventh chapter of the Book of Revelation. This is "the Revelation of Jesus Christ, ... sent and signified ... by his angel unto his servant John."[16] The following is the Word of the Lord concerning the Messengers:

> And I will give power unto my two witnesses, and they shall prophesy a thousand two hundred and threescore days, clothed in sackcloth.

The two witnesses are twin flames who come forth in the last days as representatives of Alpha and Omega, the Father/Mother God, to teach and to demonstrate the law of Christ-mastery on both the masculine and feminine rays. They are exemplars of the Law that all twin flames are destined to fulfill.

The periods of time mentioned throughout the Book of Revelation refer to initiatic intervals. The duration of the twin flames' prophecy, therefore, is measured according to the revolutions of the electrons and the cycles of the sun. The one thousand two hundred and threescore days, making a total of three and a half years, reveal that the hierarchical position of the Messengers is at the point of the Christ between God and man (their position is that of the Christ Self of the souls evolving on the planet).

The number seven symbolically stands for man. The number three and one-half, which is half of seven, indicates that the Messengers have vowed to stand as the mouthpiece for the age—the point at which Truth passes from God to man—in order that the covenant between each man and his God might be fulfilled, as Above, so below.

The phrase "clothed in sackcloth" indicates that the Messengers are not without karma, for they must bear witness to the truth that even those who have karma can become the Christ.

These are the two olive trees, and the two candlesticks standing before the God of the earth.

In the mystical sense, the two olive trees and the two candlesticks are a part of every man. They are the masculine and feminine poles focusing through the sympathetic and cerebral-spinal nervous systems in the physical body. In the universal sense, the two olive trees and the two candlesticks represent the peace and the light that their Christ Selves bring to all twin flames.

Thus they outpicture the archetypal pattern of the masculine and feminine counterparts of the Divine Mediator. In a more specific sense, they are unascended initiates appointed to serve as a liaison between ascended and unascended members of the Great White Brotherhood. The phrase "standing before the God of the earth" refers to their position in hierarchy under the Lord of the World.

> And if any man will hurt them, fire proceedeth out of their mouth, and devoureth their enemies: and if any man will hurt them, he must in this manner be killed.

The fire that proceeds out of the mouth of the Messengers is the sacred fire—the power of the spoken Word, which is theirs by reason of their holy office. This fire transmutes the energies that are directed not only against the representatives of the Christ in every age, but also against the light that passes from God to man through their mission. By the law of karma, those who intend harm against these servants of God receive quick retribution, for the power of their spoken Word is quicker than a two-edged sword.

> These have power to shut heaven, that it rain not in the days of their prophecy: and have power over waters to turn them to blood, and to smite the earth with all plagues, as often as they will.

This verse refers to the inner initiations in alchemy that the Messengers must pass in order to qualify for their office.

> And when they shall have finished their testimony, the beast that ascendeth out of the bottomless pit shall make war against them, and shall overcome them, and kill them.
>
> And their dead bodies shall lie in the street of the great city, which spiritually is called Sodom and Egypt, where also our Lord was crucified.
>
> And they of the people and kindreds and tongues and nations shall see their dead bodies three days and an half, and shall not suffer their dead bodies to be put in graves.

To qualify for the office, the Messengers must vow before the Lords of Karma to make this total sacrifice. They must be ready to surrender their life at any moment for the sake of the kingdom and the salvation of man. The Lords of Karma determine when and how that supreme sacrifice will be made.

> And they that dwell upon the earth shall rejoice over them, and make merry, and shall send gifts one to another; because these two prophets tormented them that dwelt on the earth.

Here we see the hatred that all representatives of the Brotherhood and of the Christ must be prepared to meet. It was said of the arm of the Lord that "he is despised and rejected of men"[17] (he is hated without cause). The carnal mind rejoices over the crucifixion of the Christ, for it thereby gains a temporal hold upon the consciousness of mankind.

> And after three days and an half the Spirit of life from God entered into them, and they stood upon their feet; and great fear fell upon them which saw them.
>
> And they heard a great voice from heaven saying unto them, Come up hither. And they ascended up to heaven in a cloud; and their enemies beheld them.
>
> And the same hour was there a great earthquake, and the tenth part of the city fell, and in the earthquake were slain of men seven thousand: and the remnant were affrighted, and gave glory to the God of heaven. . . .

All who would return to the consciousness of God must pass the initiations of the crucifixion, the resurrection and the ascension. Whether these rituals are performed publicly or in the temple at Luxor, they are the prerequisites to immortal life. The Messengers' ascension is a matter of akashic record, whether or not it is witnessed from the physical octave.

Whenever an ascension takes place upon the earth, the balancing action of the light raises the entire planet. Where there is discord or great density in the mass consciousness, the penetration of the light may result in cataclysm. Where the level of the mass consciousness is more spiritual, however, the action of the light produces great waves of peace that emanate throughout the four lower bodies of mankind and the earth.

It is the destiny of the Messengers of hierarchy to complete their round in the world of form and to ascend back to the Presence of God. As those who are chosen to represent the Brotherhood in every age complete their mission victoriously, so millions of others are enabled to do likewise during cycles that follow, because the Messengers have left their footprints in the sands of time.

> And the seventh angel sounded; and there were great voices in heaven, saying, The kingdoms of this world are become the kingdoms of our Lord, and of his Christ; and he shall reign for ever and ever.
>
> And the four and twenty elders, which sat before God on their seats, fell upon their faces, and worshipped God,
>
> Saying, We give thee thanks, O Lord God Almighty, which art, and wast, and art to come; because thou hast taken to thee thy great power, and hast reigned.
>
> And the nations were angry, and thy wrath is come, and the time of the dead, that they should be judged, and that thou shouldest give reward unto thy servants the prophets, and to the saints, and them that fear thy name, small and great; and shouldest destroy them which destroy the earth.
>
> And the temple of God was opened in heaven, and there was seen in his temple the ark of his testament: and there were lightnings, and voices, and thunderings, and an earthquake, and great hail.[18]

Chapter 5

The Divine Will

*Dedication to the supreme purpose
invokes the will that moves mountains.*

EL MORYA

The Divine Will

"How can I know the will of God? This is the cry of millions. Man presupposes that the Divine Will is hiding from him, as though it were a part of the plan for the Eternal God to play hide-and-seek with him. Not so! The will of God is inherent within life and merely awaits the signal of release from man's will in order to ray forth the power of dominion to the world of the individual.

"There is a sovereign link between the mortal will and the Immortal. In the statement of Jesus 'It is the Father's good pleasure to give you the kingdom,'[1] men can be aware of the eternal will as the fullest measure of eternal love.

"Release, then, your feelings of possessiveness over your own life! Surrender the mean sense of sin and rebellion, the pitiful will to self-privilege that engenders bondage.

"See the will of God as omnipresent and complete, the holy beat of the Sacred Heart throbbing within your own. Know and understand that surrender is not oblivion but a point of beginning and of greater joy. Now responsibility does not cease but begins anew, and man is yoked with eternal purpose—the shield of God's will."[2]

This is the message of El Morya, Lord of the First Ray of God's will,* "to the builders who seek Truth." Most of our readers would agree that among the gifts of life's opportunity to man there is none greater than freedom. But do most of them know that the will of God is the sole source of man's freedom?

Indeed, the sanctity of the will is shared and treasured by the wise and the ignorant among men, who seldom pause to consider what a precious gift they have in their hands.

Not My Will, but Thine, Be Done!

To surrender this will to another is to exhibit confidence of the first magnitude. There is something about holding the reins of life within one's own hands that gives men a special feeling of security, and this is as it should be. Yet we must acknowledge that there are times when an intelligence higher than our own is needed to guide the will, and there are times when the surrender of the will to that intelligence becomes desirable.

The declaration of Jesus "Nevertheless not my will, but thine, be done"[3] would be difficult for some to affirm. Those who have faith in God find it easier to surrender the will than those who yet entertain subtle doubts concerning his existence.

Hence, surrender of the personal will to the Divine is indicative not only of an abiding faith in the wisdom of God but also of a deep dedication to his purposes and a childlike trust in his unfailing love. The sweet surrender to the will of God gives man a serenity and a confidence that he can never know as long as he remains tethered to the human will with

---

*Master Morya has liberally poured out his heart's love for the will of God on many occasions. Throughout this chapter, we will weave his practical wisdom and incisive direction into the text, often attributing his quoted thoughts to him only in the notes.

its stubbornness, its misconceptions and its fears.

Says El Morya: "The fiat 'Not my will, but thine, be done' was not intended as a statement of sacrifice but one of heavenly-inspired wisdom. In the higher schools, this mantra of the Spirit is intoned invocatively so as to create the needed liaison between man and God. Whereas it is God's will that man intune with him, it is incumbent upon man to recognize that his responsibility demands search, willingness and an understanding of the self-created barriers that must be taken down so that the clarity of the will of God can come through."[4]

The God Meru gave this mantra to the students in a dictation, and it may be repeated by all who seek to do and to become God's will:

> Not my will!
> Not my will!
> Not my will, but thine, be done![5]

The Right Use of Free Will

Men are often faced with difficult choices in this valley of decision. And life will not always wait for them to make up their minds. Often a sudden demand will tax a man's entire resources. His total assets of mind, body and spirit are summoned into the decision-making process, and the decision he makes may well determine the course of his own life and the lives of millions.

Archangel Michael says, "Give me your faith and I will give you mine."[6] He knows that in times of testing, men of strong faith are not lacking in spiritual resources. These can and do rally to the occasion. But those who are without faith are often left stranded high and dry upon a desert island where they have isolated themselves.

We would agree with Saint Germain, who says, "The right use of free will is the essential difference between the spiritually exalted ones and those who are constantly whirled in a maelstrom of confusion."[7]

It is folly for anyone to deny the existence of God, of a Master Presence with a master plan who has conceived and brought into manifestation a universe of such vast precision and immutable harmony that it defies the explanation of cause and effect as accidental happenings.

Morya asks: "What shall we say, then, to the careless ones who demand their own definitions and their definitions of definitions? We will say with God, 'I AM *Āgam*, the Unknowable. I AM the Infinite within who, in all of your winnings, can never be contained within the consciousness of sense or of perception.'

"Therefore the Law of love would bestow upon man the means to contact and to know the will of God.

> "It is an inward sense
> We must discover and impart,
> It is an inward sense
> That rends the veil before we start.
> We must convey our love to him
> Who gives to us the grace to win,
> The power to see the flow of Truth,
> The sweetest comfort, eternal youth,
> And mighty power of light to live—
> This is the radiance God does give.
> In kindred minds he will impart
> The holy will of God to start
> The process over once again.

"And thus we show that the will of God is a seed to be planted within the consciousness of the individual, that the will of God is substance, even as faith is, and that the will of God is the conglomerate stream of reality—the issuance of purpose from the uncreated realm into the realm of the created essence."[8]

Just as the Divine Will has determined the course of the universe, so the free will of man has determined the course of man's existence. It is indeed in the correct and incorrect use of the will that men and women, as well as nations and peoples, have determined the course of human events.

Byways of Unreality

The channels carved by the collective will of the race determine the course of the flowing river of life. Whether you build a dam or a dike, divert the course of a stream or a river, or bottle the water and send it away, the waters of life will always follow the channels you select.

Chaos at any level is fed by the idiosyncrasies of men—their indecision, their inability or their unwillingness to cope with the mandates of their karma, their intolerance of one another's shortcomings and their habitual misapplication of life's basic principles. These have taken their toll upon the great mainstream of God's energy, which has flowed freely from the fount of life for the building of an abundant golden-age civilization.

In ignorance men have diverted the stream of life, and they have wasted the natural resources that were their birthright. In so doing they have rejected the great privilege of making straight the way that leads to the fount of life—to the I AM Presence.

As Morya says: "For far too long man has yielded his birthright unto the false, the insecure and the transitory. But when he pauses to think of his Source, there should come to mind the best gifts of life—the ever-present thoughtfulness of

God about his rate of progress, his advancement, his endowment, his protection and his ultimate fulfillment."[9]

Lord Himalaya expresses the same thought: "The best-laid plans of men must ultimately go astray unless they coincide with God's will. This is not a dictatorship; this is not even compulsion—it is the Law in action. If man had not been given the freedom to choose between his own course and the will of God, perfection would now be manifesting everywhere on earth.

"The fact that it does not is proof enough for those who require it that God has given free will to men. Only men of good will can return the gift to God by loving obedience and eternal determination!"[10]

The Master Jesus was one of these. Facing the crucifixion on the morrow, he knelt in prayer in the garden of Gethsemane. His was no ordinary consciousness revolving around a few individuals, a community or a nation. The Master's orbit was the universe, and his involvement as well as his commitment was with all of the people of this system of worlds. For upon his victory rested the fate of generations and worlds unborn.

In complete awareness of that which was to take place, the Master knew the sorrows that would come to those who sought to follow in his footsteps. Hence, he sweat "as it were great drops of blood."[11] His life energy poured out in the agony of his crucifixion for a suffering world, and the drama was played on the stage of the entire human consciousness.

At this moment of final testing, his impassioned fervor cried out in communion with the Father, with the Spirit of life everywhere: "Father, if thou be willing, remove this cup from me: nevertheless not my will, but thine, be done."[12]

The consecration of the Master's life was apparent in the singular devotion that he expressed in his hour of trial. And while it was no doubt the greatest of all tests, he met it according to the pattern of obedience to the will of God that had marked his entire mission.

It was, therefore, the capstone to a temple already builded without hands—not according to the human will but made after the Divine, eternal in the heavens. His passing of this test was the crowning achievement in his life's mission; for the triumph of the Spirit over the flesh was, is and always will be the triumph of man's obedience to the will of God.

Many admire the Master, even as many admire those who have achieved in various fields of human endeavor. But in the eyes of the Master the greatest gift that the aspirant can offer to honor his name is the gift of emulation, the gift of following in his footsteps, of not only calling him "Lord," but also of giving obedience and heed to his words and direction. Did he not say, "If ye love me, keep my commandments"?[13]

The Imitation of Christ

Pointing to the fact that man can become godlike (that he can actually experience the transfiguration of his consciousness as Jesus did) by patterning his thoughts after the Divine, El Morya asks, "If man thinks God's thoughts, are they ineffective because he is man?"[14] We know that the thoughts of God are a power in and of themselves, monads of his universal consciousness, seeds of his universal will.

When held in the heart of man God's thoughts produce after their kind, and they transform man's will according to the patterns of the Divine Will. In answering Morya's question, then, we must admit that God's thoughts when held by man (the *mani*festation of God) are just as effective as when they are held by God.

The imitation of Christ is an important aspect of discipleship that, when faithfully practiced, will lead the pure in heart to the place where they will become the Christ and where they will be able to repeat his triumphant words "Nevertheless not my will, but thine, be done."[15]

Serapis Bey, the great disciplinarian, teaches this principle to the candidates at Luxor in this wise: "Just as an actor may speak the lines of a play and enter into the identity of a living or a historical figure without ever becoming that individual, so mankind in the outer court of the temple may do homage in honest imitation of Christ-radiant men of past and present ages.

"But imitation (unless the imitator becomes the one imitated) is no substitute for the actual vesting of the God-reality of the elect upon the radiant 'light-form' that is man's blessed gift of opportunity. Descending from the heart of his own Divine Presence, this light-form is intended to be the magnificent design for his entire world; and so it becomes when the outer consciousness sustains the perfection of God's energy by vesting it with the impressions of reality."[16]

It is expected that candidates for the ascension will not only imitate the Christ but that they will also become the Christ by putting on the light-form, the magnificent design of their identity, and by consciously qualifying it with God's pure thoughts about man—"the impressions of reality."

Only One Mind, Only One Will

Scarcely able to recognize the presence of the LORD, men (out of habit) rebel at the thought of conforming to the will of God, much as they would rebel against conformity to human patterns. At all costs they must preserve their freedom to "do their thing," they say, and above all they must not be conformists to any standard except their own.

Men often feel that obedience is sacrifice, that religion is an imposition, that it binds them against their will, that it demands more than they are willing to give and that the service that is asked of them puts a damper on their personal happiness.

Knowing that Jesus exacted of his disciples the highest service to their fellowmen and obedience to the laws of God as testimony of their love for the Christ, "why do men set up a counterfeit will and call it their own? Why do they engage in a continual struggle between the will of God and 'their own' will? In the answers to these questions is to be found the key to happiness for every part of life."

Morya would have us lovingly embrace the will of God: "When man understands that there is no need to struggle for a personal existence outside of God (because he is complete in God) and that, in actuality, there are not two wills—the will of man and the will of God—but only the will of Truth and freedom, inherent within the very Spirit of Life that is the Spirit of God, then he will enter into the new sense of harmony and grace."[17]

If a man can reeducate his vision to behold the totality of his life's expression as the handiwork of God created as a thrust for a noble purpose, he will see that in reality the greatest sacrifice that he can make is to sacrifice the Higher Self to the lower self. This happens each time the human will is asserted in preference to the Divine.

You Can Fulfill Your Destiny

"The will of man is not capable of expanding self or substance, but dedication to the supreme purpose invokes the will that moves mountains. Man can do the will of God without knowing it, but by being conscious of himself as a part of the will of God he is able to fulfill his destiny in a more sublime way.

"The talents and opportunities of life are given to man as stepping-stones toward spiritual achievement, and spiritual achievement is the only goal that is real, hence worthwhile. Eternal life can best be enjoyed spiritually, for 'flesh and blood cannot inherit the kingdom of God.'[18]

"The form maker, who is the form breaker, can also be the form remaker. No loss can occur when one serves the eternal will, for the revelation of the will of God shows the seeker the abundant face of reality. One glimpse has been sufficient for many avatars, who were thereby exalted out of the socket of contemporary worldliness into positions of universal service and love.

"The greatest boon comes to those who surrender willingly with or without understanding, but always in the confidence of a faith that observes the universe and its myriad wonders and grasps with the simplicity of a child the reality of universal science. Known by any name, God is still the Creator-Father of all life, and his will bears the fashion of acceptance by all of the emissaries of heaven."[19]

Forgiveness Is the Will of God

But what happens to those who refuse to surrender their will to God, to those who continue day in and day out to sacrifice the fruits of holiness and the essence of the soul to the Moloch of human pride and to the nets of social conformity in exchange for the fickle plaudits of men and the nod of mortal approbation?

These are excluded (because they have excluded themselves) from the hallowed circle of God's consciousness. Outside the walls of the Holy City they dance and play and make merry. Seemingly oblivious to the opportunities within, they do not even notice when the sons of God pass through their midst.

But all the while they are using God's energy to bring forth images that are ungodly.

How long will the Creator endure their folly? When will the form maker break those forms and remake them after the image of the Divine? Does man's free will give him immunity from the law of recompense, or will his soul be eternally damned? The scriptures declare, "The soul that sinneth, it shall die."[20]

Is there no escape from the law of sin or from the judgments of heaven, no proviso for the return of the prodigal that his soul might not become a castaway? How does God see the pitiful plight of man, if indeed he sees it at all?

In order to answer the questions we have raised, "it is necessary that we establish in consciousness the concept of origins, for the majority of men's thought processes are patterned after the swing of the mind—to and fro. This pendulum motion, often stemming from the restlessness of men's emotions, is part of mankind's struggle for that identity which has already been bestowed upon them. But such movement can only swing men away from the peace of God and from his love.

"Let men who would discover the will of God realize that it is already a part of the universe; that the universe, in the macrocosmic sense, is already the perfection of God; and that each star, each cell and each atom was stamped with the divine image.

"The words 'Thou shalt have no other gods before me' show the necessity for the Godhead to counteract the travesty of man's acceptance of fiats of imperfection. These have been issued by lesser minds and by the deceitful ones who are self-deceived."[21]

Let us see how he will do this and yet preserve the soul of man for another day.

"In the Great Forever, in the beginningness of all things,

God saw light and he was light. Out of his light went forth the beauty of loving purpose, and in him was no darkness at all nor could there be darkness there. This was the inviolate will of God—the same yesterday, today, and forever.[22]

"The knowledge of good and evil, of duality, of the temporal and opposing factions that were within the range of the free will of the person—these came forth first as possibility and then as the looming shadows of karmic violation and disobedience to good will.

"The tenets of brotherhood were clearly stated in the golden rule: Do unto others as you would have them do unto you.[23] But each violation produced its correspondent blot, its stain upon the page, and the Lords of Karma spoke: 'This departure from the Law of Good is but a repetition of the voices sent forth unto discord.' But there was an overthrust, a compulsion of the will of God, that sought to teach by the chastening of the Law, thus to avoid the repetition of error.

"The necessity of the will of God was clear. But while perfect love casts out all fear, for fear has torment,[24] what should be done for the impoverished ones, those who had lost their perfect love from the beginningness of God?

"'Let them at least,' said the Great Ones, 'understand that God chastens those whom he loves,[25] and that he continues to love out of the bounty of his forgivingness.'

"Thus the will of God toward forgiveness was born in the consciousness of man. It was a step toward the regaining of perfection; for as men understood that as they had sowed so should they reap,[26] a desire to have perfection arose within them. This desire to return to perfection through grace became the second corollary of the will of God.

"Now the children of men who had erred saw the need to correct the error of their ways and thus be restored to the old boundaries of perfection—the perfection of perfect love. The children of the sun, who came forth bearing the white stones from the Temple of the Sun, evoked the mightiest response possible from the hearts of men; for in the hearts of men there was also a residual memory of the olden days when the elder race communed with the living God.

"Forgivingness, they saw, was eternal grace and the fire of purpose. Forgiveness, too, was the will of God. Thus the desire to return to perfect love flashed forth anew.

"'Consider the lilies of the field; they toil not, neither spin.' The cadences of the Master's words were dripping with the fires of that perfect love that is his perfect will."[27]

Thus the assayers of men's souls came into prominence. The Lords of Karma were elevated to their service, and the disposition of the will of God upon the planet took on a new note—the note of mercy, extended as opportunity, that man might return to the scene of his karma to reinvoke the will of God and to reestablish the patterns of perfection that he had lost. Mercy—the love of the will divine... how magnificent is the givingness of God!

Requirements of the Law of Mercy

According to the plan of mercy, the soul of man need not become a castaway. The prodigal may return to a state of grace, and he may reclaim his divine inheritance. But the requirements of the Law of mercy must be met. When, dear reader, they shall say to you, "Tell us what are these requirements," tell them simply so that none will feel that going home is an impossible dream.

(1) First, the errant son, determined to forsake the error of his ways, must go before his own God Presence and ask forgiveness for having departed from the path of righteousness (from the right use of God's energies and his laws).

(2) Then he must surrender his human will unconditionally to the Divine and renew his vow to serve God with his total being.

(3) Next he must invoke the violet transmuting flame through his consciousness and through his imperfect creations. The flame will requalify the energies he has misused with their original purity, in order that he may reuse these same energies to fulfill his vows and for such noble purposes as are in keeping with the will of God.

(4) Then he must go forth in love and in wisdom to do the will of God in service to his fellowman, and he must daily keep the flame of the Holy Spirit blazing on behalf of the evolutions of this planet.

Simply put, this is the path of overcoming and attainment that leads to Christhood.

Then, dear reader, if they understand the simplicity of the Law, tell them the teachings of the Master Serapis on the subject of forgivingness, as it is understood in the heart of God's flaming purity:

"When Jesus said, 'Father, forgive them; for they know not what they do,' he spake of the multitudes who passed through the wide gate. The narrow gate must exclude the paltry errors of men, but they must be willing to recognize the fact that they have erred and to come to that contriteness of heart whereby we can impart to them safely and in divine measure the commands of the Infinite over the finite mind and being. The psalm of David 'The LORD is my shepherd; I shall not want. He maketh me to lie down in green pastures: he leadeth me beside the still waters. He restoreth my soul'[28] shows clearly in its comforting vocalization that the soul must be *restored* to its original divine image.

"Many men and women are not actually aware that the soul has been swept away from its eternal moorings. They feel that the soul has been temporarily lost and that of necessity some thaumaturgic process, spiritual formula, or doctrine of salvation must be accepted and put to use by their lifestreams in order that they might obtain their eternal freedom.

"They seek, therefore, for a religion with a pattern that they can accept which will provide for them, for all time to come, both forgiveness of sins and the gift of divine grace. Men do not realize that they themselves have lost their way and that it is they who must therefore find it again. They do not realize that their specific consciousness is involved in this losing of the way and that the consciousness which they have lost is the consciousness of the Divine One that they must personally regain.

"No litany or magical formula or even an imploration to the Deity of itself possesses the fullness of the power of realignment of the four lower bodies in conjunction with the balancing of the threefold flame. Realignment is attained through the simplicity of the Cosmic Christ Mind that ever refuses to acknowledge that it has in any way been involved in a state of consciousness beneath the dignity of Truth and the majesty of the Godhead.

"The sickening beat of clenched fists upon human chests, intended as a manifestation of abject humility to the Deity and the invocation of his mercy in time of trouble, where the true spirit of repentance is lacking are of little effect in producing the state of God consciousness and divine awareness that the Law requires. The true internal sense of Cosmic Christ identification is one of beauty and rejoicing. It is the beautiful acknowledgment and perception of the laws of love and mercy; it is the acknowledgment of the tender intent of the Deity to raise the soul up the cosmic ladder of creation. Step-by-step the way is won until each one beholds for himself the pure longing of the Spirit that seeks to become one with the created being that the Spirit has made."

Thus in pursuing the requirements of the Law of mercy, the supplicant must come to the place where he understands that "there is no room for speculative theological argumentation in the Godhead, for God is not aware in his pure consciousness of man's frightening descent into mortal involvement. Only the Holy Christ Self has this awareness and acts to mediate, in his advisory capacity to the Godhead, the total world situation"[29] and the total karmic patterns of the overcomer.

Weaving the Seamless Garment

When man begins to build upon the foundations of the Divine Will and its purposes, he opens the door to admit the Master Weaver into his world. Then as the great shuttles of his life's energies flow to and fro, the seamless garment will be woven and the fabric of his soul will expand to envelop the world.

The lure of the pleasures of the senses and the desire for self-importance are traps into which the multitudes have fallen. When dealing with the human ego, there is a razor's edge that must be understood if men are to function within the framework of a practical perspective.

If the ego lacks incentive, individuals are often unable to do good work. On the other hand, the undisciplined ego left to its own devices will parade its virtues before men and stifle the creative expressions of the soul in its outreach for spiritual progress.

There is a solution for those who are unable to surrender totally by a single act of the will. It is to replace, gradually, the undesirable qualities of the human ego with the desirable qualities of the Divine Ego.

Let them take up the offer of the heavenly hosts to exchange their hatreds and their fears for God's love, their stubbornness and their perversions for his masterful control, their ignorance and greed for his illumination, their bigotry and pride for his divine direction, their disappointments and disillusionments for his vision of hope, their criticism and their misconceptions for the purity of his Truth, their defeats and backslidings for his victory, their sense of lack for his abundance and their disquietude for his peace.

Little by little, even cautiously, the individual turns over the reins of his consciousness to the Higher Self until, through the process of spiritual assimilation, his entire being is molded in the pattern of the light-form. By using this method the sense of struggle is avoided, and the violent reactions common to a dying ego do not manifest. For the transformation is so gradual that the ego, although it has given its consent, is not conscious of the fact that it is being displaced.

The Birth of the Divine Ego

Sometimes the fear of total surrender to the will of God comes from the mistaken idea that man's ego will be lost as a bubble in the ocean. And it is feared that once the ego is lost, it will never be recovered. Let all learn that even more to be feared than the loss of the ego is the fattening thereof, for there is no greater tyrant than an unbridled ego.

The ego that has not submitted itself to the Christ will make demands upon one's total resources without ever returning an iota of benefit to the individual. The finite self, while laying claim to the treasures of the soul, will begrudge the time it spends in the pursuit of the things of the Spirit—which pursuit, while it will surely strip him of his human ego, will also bring him the greatest development of his Higher Self, his Real Ego.

Jesus diagrammed the dilemma of the human ego versus the Divine Ego when he said with utter simplicity, "Whosoever shall seek to save his life shall lose it; and whosoever shall lose his life shall preserve it."[30]

Those who still believe that the surrender of their free will means the giving up of their freedom should stop and think: Freedom is a quality of God! Did not the apostle say, "Where the Spirit of the Lord is, there is liberty"?[31] Freedom is our divine prerogative, even as freedom is our divine inheritance.

The Luciferian idea that in order to gain his freedom man must rebel against a tyrannical God is the lie that has confused the issues of man's entire existence and his reason for being. This is the lie that was spawned in order to make mankind lose the remembrance of the intimate and beautiful relationship that has always existed between Father and son.

Men fear the loss of their personal identity. But did not Paul say to the Colossians, "For ye [referring to the human ego] are dead, and your life is hid with Christ in God"?[32] If the individuality of the Real Man is "hid with Christ in God," then man will find himself only by plunging into the being of God—and there in the flaming center of the Spirit of the LORD, he will find his true freedom.

The man who has surrendered himself unto God need never express a weak and palpitating human will. Nor should he express a weak and palpitating Divine Will, for the Divine Will is the strength of the Creator himself. Therefore, with certainty let men clasp the hand of the will of God as though they clasped one another's in the dark—and let them know that God's hand will lead them to the light of understanding, which surpasses all outer knowledge gained through the five senses.

The man who has surrendered himself to God knows that "the dream, the 'impossible' dream, becomes the reality. And all that man has thought to be real, insofar as his own relationship with the universe goes, is seen as a chimera—a shimmering illusion that comes from misqualified energy. In its place, in the place of the mirage of carnal identity with its shifting sands of manifestation, the reality of the Christ-identity is seen as the will of God."

And he says to himself, "What difference does it make that there are opposing forces? The forces of light are more dominant, the forces of light are greater, the forces of light are complete and eternal. They will stand when men are but dust and their present thoughts hollow echoes in the chambers of memory."[33]

After all is said and done, he comes to the realization that "Not my will, but thine, be done" is a fiat for all men. He sees that it does not mean the destruction of the human person; on the contrary, it can mean the construction of the divine person and the illumination of his actions in the light of the will of God.

Fit for the Kingdom

Illumination should always precede right action, for confidence begotten of spiritual understanding assists man in becoming one-pointed in his service. One-pointedness is a necessary virtue that should be invoked by those who would succeed on the path of service.

Those who develop singleness of mind and purpose will not be distracted by the world's thoughts, which beat at the door of self to test each man and see if he will go here and go there in search of the kingdom that is within. To those who desired to follow him, Jesus said, "No man, having put his hand to the plough, and looking back, is fit for the kingdom of God."[34]

Kuthumi echoes the sentiments of Jesus when he says: "Surrender must be beyond recall. Those who hold back part of the treasure and pleasure of life, those who still desire to live exclusively for themselves, fail to understand the Law of sweet surrender. Does man surrender to God? Can God do more than surrender in return? Can he fail to recognize that the soul has offered herself in service of the King? Shall not the King, then, empower her as his representative, as his ambassador? Shall not the King fight all of her battles and, by the spirit of absolute justice, provide her with all of her rewards?"[35]

When temptations come (and come they will, if the initiate is to advance in the order of hierarchy), he must cry out with a loud voice and with the full authority of his being say, "Get thee behind me, Satan."[36] Thus he will be following in the footsteps of the Christ, who overcame the world.

To challenge the stranger at the gate (in the name of the I AM Presence) is in keeping with the code of the Brotherhood, for a true emissary of God is never unwilling to show his credentials (his light)—whereas the gray ones will take on an injured air and belittle the one who rightfully demands proof that they are all that they claim to be.

Invariably, the needs of the world will assert themselves before the aspirant for spiritual illumination. These will pull upon his time and energy through family, friends and the poor in spirit—who are always there, looking for someone to carry their karmic burden. Worldly opportunity will knock not once but many times—even as the opportunity to glorify the self in some new and glamorous religious experience.

The prophecy of the Christ must be remembered: "For there shall arise false Christs, and false prophets, and shall shew great signs and wonders; insomuch that, if it were possible, they shall deceive the very elect."[37]

His admonishment "Wherefore if they shall say unto you, Behold, he is in the desert; go not forth: behold, he is in the secret chambers; believe it not. For as the lightning cometh out of the east, and shineth even unto the west; so shall also the coming of the Son of man be"[38] shows clearly that the coming of the Christ to the consciousness of man will occur with the swift and sudden penetration of the diamond-shining Mind of God. And he will come, not through another's attainment, but through the doorway of the receptive heart.

In the Book of Revelation we read: "He that is unjust, let him be unjust still: and he which is filthy, let him be filthy still: and he that is righteous, let him be righteous still: and he that is holy, let him be holy still."[39]

This passage indicates that the doorway to that which men call "death" is not necessarily a doorway to deification, to illumination or to progress, although we do not deny that the higher teachings can be communicated to those who are out of the body. The living Word clearly declares that those passing through the gate at the termination of their earthly life in a filthy state may well remain in that state; those who pass through in a holy state will remain holy.

Thus the will of God has ordained our best and surest means to progress in the here and now, rather than in the hereafter. The set of our sails today, the set of the rudder of life, determines the course of our ship for a long time to come. Whether men live once or through many embodiments, it is between the lines of birth and death that they must be concerned with the progress they can make as individuals in the fulfillment of their reason for being.

It is in this life, and not in the next, that they must bear in mind the words "Not my will, but thine, be done." We know that time will one day run out for all. Therefore what we do, think, say and feel, and what we are is important—because it is declaratory to our own Christ Selves, to our Divine Presence and to the Lords of Karma, as to whether or not we are really concerned with obedience to the will of God, which is the doorway to immortal life.

God instituted the change men call death as an act of

mercy that the chapters of men's existence might be terminated and they might subsequently be born again, free from the memories of the past. In the words of Kahlil Gibran, "A little while, a moment of rest upon the wind, and another woman shall bear me."[40]

Human Stubbornness

"Let men understand that it is not the Father's will that they should perish but that they should have abundant life.[41] When we begin to examine the great thoughts of God and the great will of God, when we begin to examine how great God is, we must see that cardinal to his greatness is the abundant life, the life that is eternal.

"It is fear—fear of death and fear of illusion—that has caused some men to fail to hold themselves in that state of consciousness wherein the will of God could manifest through them. They need to understand the very naturalness of cosmic purpose: God is life. They are manifesting temporal life, but they also possess, here and now, the seeds of eternal life in the very essence of the soul that God has given to them.

"The flaming Presence that directs them from above, their beloved God Presence, 'I AM,' represents the fire of the will of God; and the will of God includes within itself the all-chemistry of cosmic purpose. Therefore, each department of life is brought under the direction of the central purpose of the will of God"[42] when man surrenders his will to God.

There is nothing more degrading to the soul than the perverted human will. Conversely, there is nothing more ennobling to the soul than the magnificent Divine Will. Time and again human beings have rebelled against the will of God and even against the will of their neighbors, when they knew that the stand their neighbors took was representative of his will.

Human stubbornness is a perversion of the will of God. Human stubbornness is not a commodity that you can exchange for reality just when you are ready. Even as the snake sheds its skin, so man out of the fruit of divine wisdom would be very wise to shed stubbornness and substitute for it spiritual determination, constancy and steadfastness in service of the will of God.

"The human will presupposes that it has the knowledge which it does not have. It bases most of its choices on human history and the observations of those whose own quality of observation is centered primarily around the physical and is seldom involved with the celestial.

"The human will identifies with the ego and seeks to support it in its passing aims. Men erect monuments to their vanities that endure in substance far beyond the tenure of their own times. But we are concerned with monuments of the Spirit.

"The will of God assures man that he will survive, for it is the will of God that those whom he has created should inherit his kingdom—but the rules of the game must be followed, for the Law of God is inexorable in its demands for perfection.

"Humans, cast in the role of imperfection, have been willing to discount the possibility of their attaining that measure of perfection which stems from God-realization. Let not your hearts be troubled, for with God all things are possible.[43]

"It is just as easy to serve the will of God—in fact it is far easier—than it is to serve the decaying will of man with its varying standards. The human will propels men to false aspirations at a dizzying rate of ascent and leaves them stranded without spiritual knowledge to plummet to their destruction.

"I would like to postulate, then, that the majority of men have no conception at all of what the will of God is, therefore they do not really know what they are opposing. The human will opposes the Divine Will because its aims are shortsighted.

Men find it difficult to expand their thought beyond their days. They are prone to accept death as final and to identify with the physical form rather than with the spirit that gives it life.[44]...

"Would it not be wise then for man, caught in the net of illusion, to examine the purposes of God, to know them, to understand and serve these mighty purposes in order to accelerate in his own personal evolution the divine plan and to foster the architecture of heaven for all mankind?

Moral Decisions Based on the Will of God

"The problem of absolutes is always at hand—absolute Evil and absolute Good. These conditions are so remote from the average person that their concern lies not in the absolute but in the relative. They are concerned not with the question 'Is it a condition that manifests good or evil?' but when making a moral decision they ask, 'Is it relatively good or evil by comparison to other conditions, and does it represent the best choice?'

"Understanding moral values, which are valid because they are based on Truth, will help men to understand that their progress must come from their present state and move forward. Too many are obsessed with the idea of a utopian ideal, which because it is unobtainable they use as an excuse for lowered standards....

"Cultivate, then, the spirit of Truth.[45] Invite an honest analysis of situations. This will not require hours of your time when it is evoked out of an honest heart. The will of God that has already engraven his wisdom and love upon your heart will enable you to draw reasonable standards toward which you may reach.

"God will not seem so remote nor his will when men are able to envision it as an extension of their own consciousness from present standards to those that are still higher. But when men consider their own standards to be above the stars, then like an animalistic cult they grunt and groan, dance in circles, and dissipate their energies in vanity.

"We are concerned that the will of God come into fuller manifestation in the world of men. But in a relative sense, one man's idea of the will of God may be a far lower standard than it is for another. Men must realize that some have higher standards than others and that some can attain higher goals. Life is not meant to be filled with criticism and condemnation, but it is an opportunity to thwart the human ego that must ultimately reflect God if it is to endure."[46]

The sweet surrender that can be felt in the declaration "Not my will, but thine, be done" does not spell an end to human choices. For God always returns control to those who surrender their all unto him, by giving them the precious opportunity to master their lives according to his precepts and his laws.

As the mother bird assists the fledgling to spread its wings and fly, so God is ever anxious for men to find that direction within themselves that he has implanted there as the treasure of his heart that they may develop and make their own.

His is a patient love; we call it mercy. He gives it to all. It is a quality that is never strained except by men who misappropriate God's patient love. The Father has no desire to usurp the free will of his children by intruding his assistance and counsel where these are not sought—and if he were to do so, he would be abrogating his own Law.

It is not his will that any should perish in the degradation of the misuse of their own human will, but neither is it his intent to control his children as puppets on a string. If this were his will, he would long ago have asserted it, for he who framed the universe certainly has the power to do so.

The Return to the Divine Will

God withholds from his children the full potential of his energies until they demonstrate their willingness to be obedient to his will. This is the altogether natural attitude of a father who does not allow his children to play with fire until they have learned to use it constructively.

God asks man to surrender his will unto him only until man can demonstrate, by his assimilation of and attunement with Cosmic Law, that he has put on the Father's own understanding of divine justice. Only then is God assured that man will use his will and his power to implement the universal intent, not only for the benefit of self and others but also for the benefit of all cosmos.

He who withholds his human will from surrender to the Divine Will but hinders his own entering into the kingdom and stays a little the progress of the whole world that waits daily for the sunrise. The greatest sunburst of all life is the will of God, which is indeed good for everyone.

His will trembles with the joy of the whole capsule of identity, full of grace and happiness. Without being centered in the will of God both within and without, man loses the meaning of his life and it vanishes—even as a waning moon falls beyond the horizon, leaving no shimmering trail upon the waters.

"The flashing forth of the renewal of the first covenant is the will of God; for it was this bond to which every soul who received the gift of individual life expression did once consent. The breaking of the bond of God's will has meant the parting of the way between father and son. For the prodigal son has chosen to wander into the depths of maya to seek his fortune in the realm of illusion.[47]

"Now we say, let us return to reality, to the Father and to the heavenly will. Thus shall the fire purify each man's work and the fiery trial cease in a pact of friendship with God."[48]

"Long has the soul been dead
  In the night of personal delusion—
  The struggles, the accumulated karmic debts,
  And the great harms.
  Now the end has come
  In one solemn sweet surrender:
  I AM—Thou art—we are—
  All are One!"[49]

Chapter 6

Planes of Consciousness

*Life unfolds its wealth and beauty
according to the unveilment or expansion
of consciousness. . . .*

*You see yourself as small and limited. . . .
But when you close your eyes in meditation,
you see the vastness of your consciousness—
you see that you are in the center of eternity.
Concentrate there.*

PARAMAHANSA YOGANANDA

Planes of
Consciousness

Cosmic energy-spirals of God's consciousness, cascading from the Great Central Sun over the crystal cord, pass through the individualized I AM Presence and the Christ Self. They spring up as a threefold flame fountain within the heart chalice, whence they flow to myriad pools of light in the being of man. These pools or radiating centers, called "chakras," are the foci for the distribution of God's energy to the four lower bodies of man.

We shall also refer to the chakras as crystal chalices, for although they have a whirling action (*chakra* is a Sanskrit word meaning "wheel"), they also function as receptacles for the crystal waters of the river of life that flows from God to man and from man to God.

The terms "chakra" and "chalice" are used interchangeably because it is important that students develop the "grail consciousness" when meditating upon these centers, even while they visualize the whirling action of the sacred-fire wheels. The centers should, therefore, be thought of first as cups consecrated to contain the pure essence of the Holy Spirit, then as wheels within wheels focusing the power of the Great Central Sun Magnet in the microcosmic world of man.

The chart on the following page describes the seven major crystal chalices. They are anchored in the etheric body in a straight line parallel to the spine. The first column in the chart gives their English and Sanskrit names, and the second column lists the ray intended to be released through each one. The third column shows the pure colors that the chakras emanate and the number of their petals or waves.

It should be noted that the pure colors of the chakras are often muddied by the accumulation of astral substance over them. Thus the colors may vary according to the misqualifications released through them. Some clairvoyants have seen astral colors emanating from the chakras of unascended lifestreams and have erroneously thought them to be their natural emanations. Those who wish to verify the colors of the chakras should call for the Electronic Presence of Jesus Christ to display the cosmic radiance of the chakras as they appear in his ascended light body.

The fourth column lists the seven bodies of man, whose patterns are fulfilled in the planes of Spirit and Matter through the seven chalices.[1] The chakras "flower" on the surface of the physical body opposite the organs and glands named in the fifth column. These serve as the focal point in the physical body for the specialized function of each of the seven major chakras. The sixth column lists the seven corresponding subchakras and their colors.

The body of man contains a total of 144 chakras. We shall not list the remaining 130. Suffice it to say that they are positioned throughout the etheric body as anchor points for the release of the 144,000 virtues that radiate from the Great Central Sun. Let us turn our attention instead to the vital functions of the seven major crystal chalices or chakras.

NAME	RAY	PURE COLOR, PETALS	BODY	RELATED ORGANS AND GLANDS	SUBCHAKRA COLOR
Crown *Sahasrara*	2	Yellow 972	I AM Presence	Cerebrum, pituitary gland, hypothalamus	Between crown and third eye Pale yellow
Third Eye *Ajna*	5	Emerald green 96	Causal Body	Brain stem, cerebellum, pineal gland, eyes, ears	Thymus Yellow
Throat *Vishuddha*	1	Sapphire blue 16	Etheric body	Lungs, thyroid, larynx, trachea, vocal chords	Spleen Golden pink
Heart *Anahata*	3	Rose pink 12	Christ Self	Heart, thymus, lymphatic system, diaphragm	Hands Yellow with pink aura
Solar Plexus *Manipura*	6	Purple and gold, ruby flecked 10	Emotional body	Stomach, kidneys, pancreas, liver, gallbladder, adrenals	Hands Yellow with pink aura
Seat of the Soul *Svadhishthana*	7	Violet, purple, pink 6	Mental body	Spleen, ovaries, uterus, testes, intestines, appendix	Feet Yellow
Base of the Spine *Muladhara*	4	White 4	Physical body	Bladder, rectum, reproductive organs	Feet Yellow

Functions of the Chakras

The chakras serve first as transformers for stepping down the frequencies of God's energy and for the release of the four cosmic forces—fire, air, water and earth—in the planes of Spirit and Matter. The seven major chakras are conductors for the flow of energy to the seven subcenters and the remaining 130 chakras, which anchor the light of God as stars in the firmament of man's being.

In addition, God designed the crystal chalices as the open doors through which the seven rays are intended to flow from man's being—lighting his world, weaving the seamless garment, and forming the antahkarana connecting man and man, as well as man and God.

As crystals, the seven major chakras focus in the etheric body the intricate soul patterns that are to be woven in the mental, emotional and physical vehicles. As cups, they retain the pure white light that sustains the life pattern in man. Thus through the various functions that we shall discuss, the chakras serve as focal points for the interaction of the cosmic energy-spirals between the Macrocosm and the microcosm.

The Law of Giving and Receiving

The law of giving and receiving is fulfilled in man through the chalices. It is the divine intent that man qualify the white light released from his heart flame through the seven chakras with Christly virtues colored by the seven rays and vibrating in consonance with the eternal Logos.

Simultaneously, man is intended to draw in through the chalices the essence of the Holy Spirit (prana), which occurs universally as electronically charged light. Thus the balancing activities of Alpha and Omega (of giving and receiving) are intended to be fulfilled in the outbreathing and the inbreathing of light through the chalices.

Energy is released from the chalices in positive (clockwise) evolutionary spirals. Energy drawn into the chalices enters in negative (counterclockwise) involutionary spirals. The centrifugal (positive) and centripetal (negative) action that is produced when these dual processes function at maximum efficiency causes the chalices to open like flowers unfolding their petals and to spin like miniature dazzling suns.

Sparkling like diamonds as they whirl, the crystals give off an electrical charge that quickens the whole being of man, making him a veritable polestar in the transitory world.

The number of petals (or waves) in each chakra is determined by the ray, the plane and the frequency of the centrifugal and centripetal action of the intertwining plus and minus energies. These factors also produce the basket-weave effect that has been noted in the chalices. When thus fulfilling their God-intended purposes in illumined man, the chalices are convex.

In unillumined man, who still functions as part of the mass consciousness, the chakras are submerged in a sea of astral substance that prevents them from either radiating the light of the I AM Presence or drawing in the essence of the Holy Spirit for the nourishment of the four lower bodies.

In this state of nonfulfillment, the centers cannot even be called chalices. They are dull and sluggish, silvery instead of crystal, and appear as moons under the sea instead of stars in the firmament. They are concave, and their petals are not fully opened.

Subject to the ebb and flow of the tides of human emotion, and not knowing how to "breathe out" the light of the Presence nor how to "breathe in" the essence of the Holy Spirit, unillumined man turns to the stimuli of the world to keep his centers and his four lower bodies energized.

Misusing the negative spirals in the chakras, he substitutes the drawing in of astral energies for the drawing in of the essence of the Holy Spirit. Misusing the positive spirals, he spews out from his chakras the perversions of the seven rays and the Christly virtues, discoloring his aura and contaminating his planetary home.

The Release of Light through the Chakras

When man allows the seven rays and their Christly virtues to flow through his chakras, God's energy as lines of force is sustained as highways of light between himself and his God Presence.

For instance, the golden ray of illumination, after it is released through the crown chakra, circles the earth in a clockwise spiral following the ritual of creation. As man qualifies the stream of energy flowing through his crown chakra with the purity of wisdom's ray, it is amplified according to the intensity of his devotion to the flame.

As it circles the earth, this energy-spiral makes a complete cycle through the four lower bodies of the planet, passing through the planes of fire (etheric), air (mental), water (emotional) and earth (physical), gathering through the law of attraction energies of like vibration. Then it ascends via the counterclockwise figure-eight pattern, according to the ritual of sublimation, to the second band in the Causal Body—the gold or yellow band, to which it corresponds in color and virtue.

The energies released from the six remaining chakras follow the same rituals of creation and sublimation—circling the earth, cycling through the four planes and then ascending to the Causal Body.

The brilliant emerald-green ray of precipitation is released through the third eye as the vision and vitality of man's abundant creations. The sapphire-blue ray of the will of God is released through the throat chakra as the power of the spoken Word, to coalesce in form the blueprint of the life pattern held in the etheric body. The pink ray of divine love is released through the heart chalice as the fire of love that binds the creation through the consciousness of the Christ Self.

The purple-and-gold ray of ministration and service is released through the solar plexus as the flow of peace that weaves the etheric patterns into the emotional body. The violet ray of freedom, transmutation and forgiveness is released through the seat of the soul, anchoring the image of the Christ Mind in the mental body. And the white flame of purity and discipline is released through the base-of-the-spine chakra as the creative power of the I AM Presence anchored in the physical body.

The Hub of Life

To grasp the laws governing the activities of the seven rays in the seven bodies of man, we must understand the creation of man in the very center of God's androgynous consciousness, the white fire core of the Great Central Sun.[2]

Man's Causal Body is a miniature replica of the Great Central Sun. Moreover, every atom in manifestation is built upon this same pattern of energy spirals evolving spheres within spheres. The color bands of the Great Central Sun as well as of the atom are planes of God's consciousness differentiated only by their frequency, or vibration. The white fire core is the focus of Spirit becoming Matter and Matter becoming Spirit.

Thus in the hub of the Great Central Sun and in the heart of every atom, the spiritual sun and the physical sun coexist. Here in the white fire core the simultaneous manifestation of Spirit and Matter provides the necessary components for creation. Here and only here can creation take place.

Eleven concentric rings surround the core of God's being. These, together with the center, comprise the twelve planes of consciousness found in the Atom of God—seven outer rays plus the five secret rays.

The Five Secret Rays

The rings of the five secret rays are positioned between the white fire core and the yellow band of the Causal Body (figure 4, page 16). These planes do not pertain to existence as we know it upon earth but rather to man's latent divinity, which remains unrealized except by those who have risen even beyond the levels of initiation required for the attainment of Christhood.

The full knowledge and use of the secret rays by the evolutions of this world have not been authorized by the Solar Lords, who require the planetary mastery of the seven planes of the Christ consciousness through the seven color rays before the powers of the secret rays will be conferred upon evolving humanity. We can, however, invoke the Ascended Master who is known as Mighty Cosmos to release the action of the secret rays in our behalf that they will spiritualize consciousness in the planes of Matter.

The white fire core and the six spheres beyond the five secret rays are the planes that relate to the evolution of God's consciousness as humanity in their present evolution are able to experience and express it.

The planes of the secret rays are perpendicular [orthogonal] to the planes of the seven rays (figure 5).[3] For this reason they are not shown on the Causal Body in the Chart of Your Divine Self (color illustration facing page 74), although they exist as potential in the Causal Body of every son and daughter of God made in the divine likeness.

FIGURE 5: Orientation of the five secret rays.
The five secret rays, between the white and yellow bands of the
Causal Body, are perpendicular [orthogonal] to the seven rays.

The Individualization of the God Flame

The great miracle of life is that the Universal God can individualize himself within the white fire core of being at any point in space he so desires. The creation of the Divine Monad—the God-identity of the individual, his I AM Presence—takes place when the Spirit of God projects the light seed of his image into the ovoid of Matter[4] in the hub of the Great Central Sun to create a new white fire body.

Through the resulting union of the essence of Spirit and Matter (yang and yin) in the plane of Matter-earth, a miniature white fire core is formed in the heart of the Great Central Sun (figure 6a). This is the moment of the individualization of the God Flame. This is the birth of the androgynous sphere of being out of which a polar realization of wholeness is born (figure 6b).

Spirit sparks of the Deity proceed from this white-fire T'ai Chi, one assuming the masculine polarity and the other the feminine—yet in their oneness, each remains an androgynous whole (figure 6c).

These are twin flames representing the Father-Mother God. Each of these twin flames forms the nucleus of an individualized I AM Presence (figure 6d).

Then within the heart of each I AM Presence (which retains the balance of the yin and yang aspects of the Godhead), the seed of the Christ Self is sealed, born out of the union of the Alpha and Omega spirals in the white fire core (figure 6e).

To evolve as a replica of God's being, each Divine Monad —whose seed is within itself—must pass through the twelve planes of God's solar consciousness, which comprise the twelve spheres of the Great Central Sun. The Monad absorbs from the Great Central Sun that which its fiery destiny ordains. This is the unique blueprint of its evolution that is impressed upon the white fire core of the individual I AM Presence.

Although at the moment of birth the Causal Bodies of twin flames are identical (but in polarity), the subsequent evolution of the twin flames in the world of form determines what momentums accrue to their individual Causal Bodies (figure 6f). Although they pursue divergent paths of creativity, the electronic pattern of their identity remains the same.

The Bands of the Causal Body

The innermost band of the Causal Body is the white sphere. This band surrounds your I AM Presence, the white fire core of your Real Self, one with our Father-Mother God (see figure 7). Serapis Bey referred to the distinction between the white fire core of your being and the white sphere of your Causal Body when he announced a dispensation "whereby you can increase the great white sphere of your individual Causal Body surrounding the light of Alpha and of Omega."[5] The white sphere is the plane of Matter-earth.

The second sphere, the yellow band, is the plane of Spirit-earth. The third sphere, the pink band, is the plane of Spirit-fire and Matter-fire. The fourth sphere, the violet band, is the plane of Matter-air. The fifth sphere, the purple-and-gold band, is the plane of Matter-water. The sixth sphere, the green band, is the plane of Spirit-air, and the seventh sphere, the blue band, is the plane of Spirit-water.

Figure 8 gives an eye-picture of how the four cosmic forces are distributed in polarity through the upper and lower chakras. The Christ Self, acting as the mediator between Spirit and Matter, focuses the planes of both Spirit-fire and Matter-fire in the heart chakra. Born within the white fire core of God's being, the Christ becomes the hub of the microcosm. Keeping the flame between the Higher Self and the lower self, the Christ is the integrator of life where Spirit is becoming Matter and Matter is becoming Spirit.

The being of man is suspended between Spirit-earth (the crown chakra) and Matter-earth (the base-of-the-spine chakra). It is through the polarity of the Father-Mother God, anchored in these chakras as the lodestone of the Presence (crown: plus) and the seed atom (base of the spine: minus), that the being of man is sustained in form in both Spirit and Matter simultaneously.

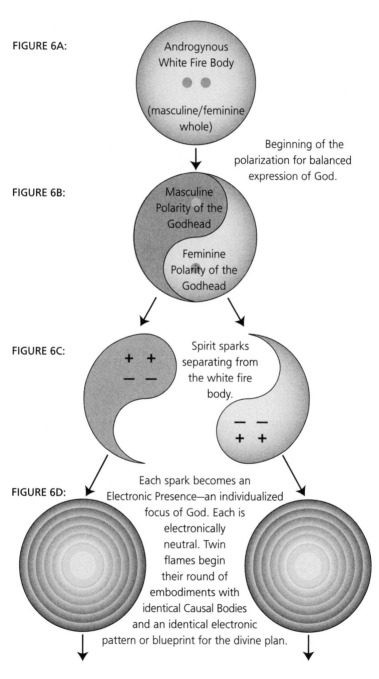

FIGURE 6: Creation of twin flames.

FIGURE 6A:

Androgynous White Fire Body

(masculine/feminine whole)

Beginning of the polarization for balanced expression of God.

FIGURE 6B:

Masculine Polarity of the Godhead

Feminine Polarity of the Godhead

FIGURE 6C:

+ +
— —

Spirit sparks separating from the white fire body.

— —
+ +

FIGURE 6D:

Each spark becomes an Electronic Presence—an individualized focus of God. Each is electronically neutral. Twin flames begin their round of embodiments with identical Causal Bodies and an identical electronic pattern or blueprint for the divine plan.

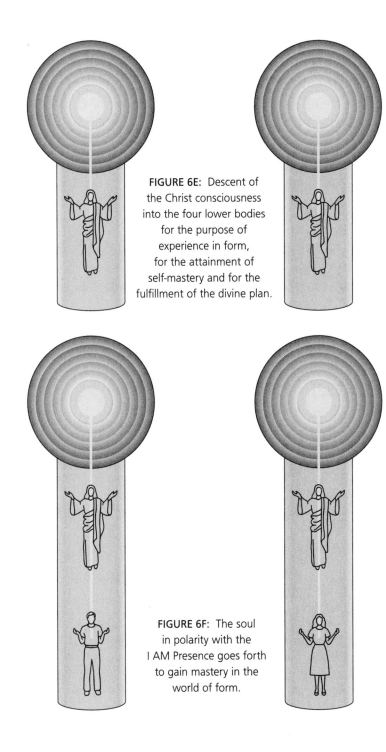

FIGURE 6E: Descent of the Christ consciousness into the four lower bodies for the purpose of experience in form, for the attainment of self-mastery and for the fulfillment of the divine plan.

FIGURE 6F: The soul in polarity with the I AM Presence goes forth to gain mastery in the world of form.

The spheres of the five secret rays are located between the planes of Matter-earth (the white band) and Spirit-earth (the yellow band). The order of the planes of God's consciousness focused within these five secret rays is the same as that of the five outer spheres of the Causal Body. That is, the first secret ray is the plane of Spirit-fire and Matter-fire, the second secret ray is the plane of Matter-air, the third secret ray is the plane of Matter-water, the fourth secret ray is the plane of Spirit-air, and

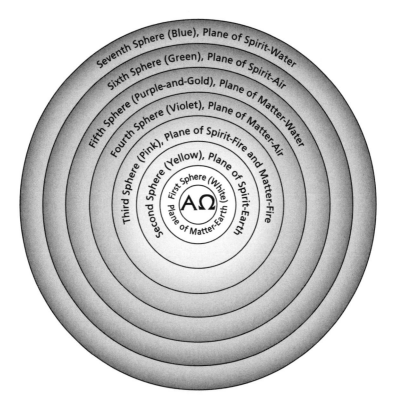

FIGURE 7: The four cosmic forces in the Causal Body.
Your I AM Presence is the white fire core of your being that establishes your union with our Father-Mother God, Alpha and Omega. The color bands, beginning with the white, hold the energy of your lifestream that you have qualified for God-good through the Spirit-Matter planes of fire, air, water and earth.

the fifth secret ray is the plane of Spirit-water.

It is precisely because the earth planes are not represented in the five secret rays that these rays represent the uncrystallized aspect of God's consciousness. This fact also explains their location between the white and yellow spheres, causing the rays to be braced between the planes of Matter-earth and Spirit-earth in the Causal Body, and enabling them to be integrated with the energy spirals of the form creation when necessary.

The relationship of the five secret rays to the seven color rays is the same as that of the notes corresponding to the black keys and the white keys on the piano. The cosmic tone, color, frequency and dimension of the secret rays is, so to speak, halfway between that of the color rays; but in position they are perpendicular to the planes of Matter-earth and Spirit-earth.

Because the planes of the seven rays are necessary for the creation of form in both Spirit and Matter, the five secret rays are incomplete without the seven color rays. This is comparable to the five black keys on the piano being incomplete without the seven white keys.

The Creation of the Causal Body

The individual Causal Bodies of twin flames are formed as each individualized I AM Presence, sealed within its own white fire body, revolves through the twelve spheres of the Great Central Sun, gathering unto itself the solar momentum of each sphere according to the pattern of its fiery destiny.

Thus layer upon layer, as the Divine Monad spirals through the twelve rings of God's Causal Body according to preordained cycles, the microcosmic world of the Divine Monad is born within the Macrocosm. As the Monad cycles through the twelve spheres of the Great Central Sun, it passes through and comes under the influence of the twelve solar hierarchies,

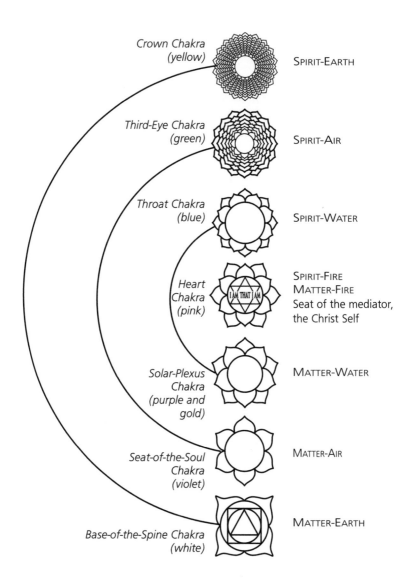

FIGURE 8: The four cosmic forces distributed in polarity through the upper and lower chakras. The Christ Self, focusing Spirit-fire and Matter-fire, acts as the mediator in man—the *mani*festation of God—where Spirit becomes Matter and Matter becomes Spirit.

adding to its Causal Body one sphere with each revolution.

The twelve flames of the twelve hierarchies, together with the seeds of the godly virtues, are magnetized within each sphere to serve as focuses for future initiations that the soul will have to pass in the world of form under their respective houses. Each of these twelve focuses also holds the pattern for twelve of the 144 chakras.

After making one complete rotation around the clock within the first sphere (the plane of Matter-earth, the origin and fulfillment of cycles of being), the Monad passes to the next sphere, which is the plane of the first secret ray.

After spiraling through the spheres of the five secret rays, one cycle within each sphere, systematically gathering unto itself the rays of the spheres and the flames of the hierarchies, the Monad proceeds through the spheres of the six remaining color rays.

The journey completed in the outermost (blue) sphere, its twelve cycles fulfilled, the creation of the Causal Body is complete. The Divine Monad is projected out from the Great Central Sun to expand the glory of life as a star in the macrocosmic body of God.

The Journey of the Soul and the Creation of the Crystal Chalices

Simultaneously, as the individualized I AM Presence spirals through the spheres of the Great Central Sun, the soul consciousness—that is, the image of the I AM Presence that is impressed upon the substance of Matter-earth—spirals through the spheres of the individualized Causal Body that are being formed. During the journey of the soul through the world of the Divine Monad, the etheric body is woven and the 144 crystal chalices are anchored within it.

Through the seven major chakras and seven subchakras

and the 130 minor chakras that come under their influence, the twelve planes of God's consciousness are anchored within the soul and its etheric envelope. This anchoring of God's consciousness in man is necessary for him to function as an integrated being in the planes of both Spirit and Matter, and for him to become a co-creator with God—lowering into the plane of Matter the fiery destiny locked within his Causal Body.

The goal of life is for man to become one with God—as Above, so below. Man must precipitate below in his four lower bodies all that God has placed as potential above in the three higher bodies (the I AM Presence, the Causal Body and the Christ Self).

By tracing the journey of the soul through the individualized Causal Body, we shall see how the 144 chakras are positioned in the etheric body, the soul receiving one chakra as it enters each of twelve "houses" in each of the twelve spheres.

Beginning in the white sphere of Matter-earth, the soul receives the base-of-the-spine chakra plus the eleven minor chakras that come under its influence. The seed atom, containing the image of the Christ (the electronic pattern of the Monad that will be stamped upon the lower vehicles), is suspended within the base-of-the-spine chakra.

The seed atom is in turn the white fire core of a miniature Causal Body that is formed around it, focusing the twelve planes of God's consciousness in the plane of Matter. The seed atom is the focus of the Divine Mother, of the feminine ray of the Godhead, which anchors in Matter the energies of Spirit.

Passing through the spheres of the five secret rays, the soul and its etheric envelope receive the focuses of those rays and the eleven minor chakras under the influence of each of the secret rays.

Proceeding to the second sphere (the yellow band), the soul and the etheric envelope receive the crown chakra, the focus of Spirit-earth and the eleven minor chakras that come under its influence.

Here in the plane of Spirit the lodestone of the Presence is anchored. A miniature replica of the white fire core of the I AM Presence, this is the focus of the Divine Father. The divine polarity of the Father-Mother God focused at the top of the head and the base of the spine assures man that he, too, has the opportunity of becoming androgynous.

The power-wisdom of the Father infusing the love-purity of the Mother produces the Christ consciousness in the heart chalice, which is anchored in the etheric body together with the eleven minor chakras, during the soul's journey through the third sphere (the pink band of the Causal Body).

Here Spirit-fire and Matter-fire function as coefficients of Spirit-earth and Matter-earth. These sacred fires produce the threefold flame—the balanced action of power, wisdom and love—the coordinates of Father, Son and Holy Spirit. Here in the center of being, the mandala of the lifestream—the flaming crystal of the Christ Self—is placed over the heart chakra to magnify the energies of the flame of life.

Next, the soul and its etheric body pass through the fourth sphere (the violet band) and receive the seat-of-the-soul chakra (the focus of Matter-air), together with the eleven minor chakras under its influence. Through this chalice the image of the Christ Mind is anchored in the mental body that it might be stamped upon the seed of both male and female (the sperm and the ovum) to carry the life pattern for incoming souls. Here the solar radiance is anchored that the divine blueprint may be manifest in Matter.

At this level the flame of freedom allows the soul to choose between the human will and the Divine Will. If it chooses the Divine, then that Mind that was in Christ Jesus will indeed be manifest in the creations of that son or daughter of God.

In the fifth sphere (the purple band tinged with gold), the soul and its etheric body receive the sun chalice, or solar plexus (the focal point for the release of the solar radiance in the plane of Matter), together with the eleven minor chakras under its influence.

Through this chakra the emotional body develops the fiery destiny of the soul in the plane of Matter-water. Great opportunity for the expansion of the fires of the soul occurs in this plane. For when properly governed, man's emotions (his energies in motion) can release a tremendous impetus for good in the world of form. Needless to say, when ungoverned they are the cause of man's undoing.

In the sixth sphere (the green band), the soul and its etheric body receive the third-eye chalice, the focus of Spirit-air. Through the vision of the All-Seeing Eye of God anchored in this chakra, man is able to lower into the planes of Spirit and Matter the patterns of his Causal Body.

Whereas these patterns are released into the planes of Matter through the seat-of-the-soul chakra and the lower mental body, they come forth in the plane of Spirit through the third eye when the consciousness has returned to the single-eyed vision of the Edenic state.

During its journey through the seventh sphere (the blue band), the soul and the etheric body receive the throat chakra, the focus of Spirit-water. When the power of the spoken Word is released through this chakra, the patterns of the etheric body become the Word made flesh.

When the soul has completed its cycles through the twelve bands of the individual Causal Body and accepts the divine mandate to descend into form, it is the power of the spoken Word that causes the essence of liquid fire (Spirit-water) to coalesce the form of the three lower vehicles according to the electronic pattern of the lifestream.

The Soul Is Clothed in "Coats of Skins"

The descent of the soul into embodiment follows the cycle of the Cosmic Clock (figure 9) as surely as the suns and stars and atoms. In the ritual of creation, the formation of the etheric body is accomplished in the fire quadrant under the direction of the hierarchies of the twelve o'clock, one o'clock and two o'clock lines.

This ritual, an activity of the planes of Spirit-fire and Matter-fire, is begun in the heart chalice of the individualized I AM Presence and the Christ Self when the soul is formed. It is completed when the soul fulfills its twelfth round through the Causal Body.

As the sheath (or mantle) of the soul, the etheric body remains intact from one embodiment to the next, retaining the impressions stamped upon it by the qualification of energy occurring in the three lower vehicles. Each time the soul takes form, the mental, emotional and physical bodies are formed anew, according to the patterns stored in the etheric body.

The higher etheric body contains the blueprint of your origin. It is God's memory of your soul pattern that is to be outpictured through the Mind of Christ. This blueprint is your reality. It is not mere intellectual knowledge. It is more than four-dimensional, and it contains the record and nature of your Electronic Presence (your I AM Presence)—the same pattern you share with your twin flame, the pattern that is focused through the seat-of-the-soul chakra in the seed and the egg of man and woman.

The lower etheric body contains the subconscious records and patterns of all of your creations in the Matter universe from all embodiments.

In each successive embodiment, the portion of the etheric body that holds the records of the soul's past lives is sealed.

174

FIGURE 9: The Cosmic Clock.

The energies of creation are released through the twelve hierarchies of the sun according to the law of cycles in a clockwise direction. Creative energy is released from God first through the etheric quadrant (fire) and then progressively through the mental quadrant (air), the emotional quadrant (water) and finally through the physical quadrant (earth).

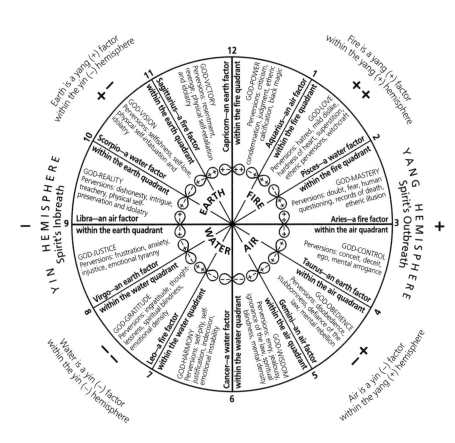

Note: The ++/−+/−−/+− notations in the infinity symbols ∞ that form the central ring are to be read from the center of the circle. As indicated around the outside of the Clock, ++ stands for fire, −+ for air, −− for water, and +− for earth. These notations are a visual representation of the information recorded on the line of the Clock that bisects the infinity symbol. For example, "Libra, an air factor..." shows −+ in the corresponding half of its infinity symbol, and "...within the earth quadrant" shows +−.

These records remain inaccessible until the soul has reached a level of attainment by which access to these records is useful to the soul's spiritual progress. However, records that are not aligned with the soul's divine plan are susceptible to violet-flame transmutation according to the law of cycles governed by the Cosmic Clock.

The immaculate conception of the soul—the divine mandate for its descent into form—and the conception of the physical body take place under the direction of the hierarchy of the three o'clock line. The formation of the mental body occurs in the air quadrant under the direction of the hierarchies of the three, four and five o'clock lines. This ritual, an activity of the planes of Spirit-air and Matter-air, is fulfilled through the third-eye and seat-of-the-soul chakras during the first three months of gestation.

The focusing of the solar radiance for the precipitation of the emotional body occurs in the water quadrant under the direction of the hierarchies of the six, seven and eight o'clock lines. This ritual, an activity of the planes of Spirit-water and Matter-water, is fulfilled through the throat and solar-plexus chakras during the second three months of gestation.

The completion of the physical body occurs in the earth quadrant under the direction of the hierarchies of the nine, ten and eleven o'clock lines. This ritual, an activity of the planes of Spirit-earth and Matter-earth, is fulfilled through the crown and base-of-the-spine chakras during the final three months of gestation.

Although the patterns of the three lower bodies are fulfilled in the manner described, they develop simultaneously during the nine-month period of gestation. By observing the positions of the twelve hierarchies and the cosmic forces they represent on each line of the Clock, we can see how the four planes of God's consciousness are woven into the fabric of the soul for the intermeshing of the four lower bodies.

During the first month of gestation the hierarchy of Aries on the three o'clock line focuses the fire element in the mental body. During the second month of gestation the hierarchy of Taurus on the four o'clock line focuses the earth element in the mental body. During the third month the hierarchy of Gemini focuses the air element in the mental body, and so on around the Clock until the moment of birth when the soul begins a new cycle of opportunity in form.

All of the twelve hierarchies of the Great Central Sun focus their particular momentum of service to the incoming soul through the hierarchy in charge of the cycle and ritual of the month.

In *Nurturing Your Baby's Soul: A Spiritual Guide for Expectant Parents*, I explained: "From the moment of conception, the child's soul is an active participant in forming the body she is to inhabit to fulfill her mission in life.

"Throughout the entire nine months of gestation, the soul may go back and forth from her body in the womb to higher planes of existence in the heaven-world. Each time the soul enters her body she anchors more of her soul substance in that body. As gestation progresses, the spirit, or the essence, of the soul becomes a part of the blood and the cells—a part of the brain, the heart and all of the organs.

"At the moment of birth, under the direction of the hierarchy of the twelve o'clock line (the timing of which is integral to the soul's mission), the soul comes down the spiritual birth canal, which is like a large funnel." This is when the threefold flame is anchored in the heart chalice.

Prior to birth the threefold flame of the mother sustains the heart and necessary functions of the fetus through the placenta and the umbilical cord, which bear a striking resemblance to the Causal Body and the crystal cord.

"The soul is fully integrated with the body at the moment of birth, and a curtain of forgetfulness is drawn over the memory body of the soul at that time. The soul then no longer has full memory of her preexistence in the heaven-world or in past lives."[6]

A Date with Destiny

All of us have a date with our destiny and with our karma. If we miss the date, then we miss our opportunity to pay off old debts that we owe certain individuals. And if we miss our cycle of opportunity, we may not get it again for a long, long time.

Mother Mary has described the frustration of souls who are not able to meet their timetables: "There are souls who have been denied life who have a tremendous anguish and frustration that they are not in embodiment to help you meet the crisis of your cities and your nations, every crisis that besets you this day. One of the principal reasons why there is such crisis is that those whom God has sent to be here when these challenges were to come upon earth are not in embodiment.... [This is] an upset of the spiritual-cosmic ecosystem."[7]

Abortion is a very controversial issue, but we are obliged to share what may be for many a new perspective on this subject—a spiritual perspective and the soul's perspective. What is the perspective of the unborn child? From the soul's point of view, the most painful and tragic consequence of abortion is that it aborts the divine plan of their soul—the special mission in life they have been waiting to fulfill, sometimes for thousands of years. Abortion also cuts short the divine plan of entire groups of souls who are tied together by their karma and cannot complete their mission because part of their "team" didn't make it into embodiment.

In addition, souls who need to reincarnate so that they can

balance their karma are finding it more and more difficult to do so. To date, at least 36 million abortions have been performed since the 1973 *Roe v. Wade* decision—an equivalent of 7.5 percent of the current U.S. population. These "missing persons" will not take their place as adults on the world scene in the twenty-first century, nor will those who might have been their offspring. The absence of these souls in embodiment in this hour has compromised the divine plan for earth.

Family planning and the use of safe contraceptives are important, but birth control begins before conception. (Abortion is acceptable when there is jeopardy to the life of the mother.) It is important to realize that many have vowed at inner levels, before taking embodiment, to sponsor certain souls by bearing them as children. Thus prayer and invocation to the will of God should always be a part of parents' decisions on family planning.

Mother Mary says, "Life begins at conception—and I speak of the conception of the soul in the heart of the Great Central Sun, of you and your twin flame in the beginning. Life on earth likewise begins at conception, and even at that moment does the spirit begin to weave itself as part of the fabric, even the warp and woof of that body. Therefore, woman has a right to bring forth that which is conceived by love and in love by God."[8]

Saint Germain adds that "a nation is vulnerable who has not defended life in the womb.... Life must become sensitive to life."[9] Those who have supported abortion have many opportunities to become sponsors of life. Saint Germain encourages all who can to provide a home for souls waiting to take their place on the stage of life. We can pray that souls who have been aborted and are waiting to incarnate will find parents to sponsor them. We can also provide support to incoming souls by sponsoring children financially or by participating in community mentoring programs. We can support or work with organizations that care for underprivileged children and help mothers to carry their babies to term and, if they do not wish to raise them, to put them up for adoption.

The Meshing of the Four Lower Bodies

The four quadrants of the Cosmic Clock represent phases of Matter, levels of energy through which the God Flame is progressively coalesced, beginning with fire and culminating in physical precipitation. These phases of Matter constitute the substance of the four lower bodies.

The trines of the Cosmic Clock are the triangles formed by connecting the lines corresponding to the same element. Thus there are four trines, corresponding to fire, air, water and earth. These represent the activity of the threefold flame qualifying the levels of Matter. They mesh to anchor the elements of man's consciousness as memory, thoughts, feelings and physical form (figure 10).

Through this activity, the fire body is directly linked to each of the other three lower bodies. So is the physical body. For all of man's lower bodies must partake of God's fire and they all exist in the realm of Matter—therefore they all take on a level of physical form.

The mental, emotional and physical bodies anchor the fire body to provide man with memory and a chalice for the divine plan, the fiery essence of his God-identity. The etheric, mental and emotional bodies anchor the physical body to provide man with physical form through which he can crystallize unique fire-blossoms of love.

But thoughts and feelings can act independently. Thus the mental and emotional bodies do not directly mesh with each other, although often they outwardly influence each other. The

180

FIGURE 10: The meshing of the four lower bodies.
The etheric and the physical bodies register the four elements.
The mental and emotional bodies register in only three planes.

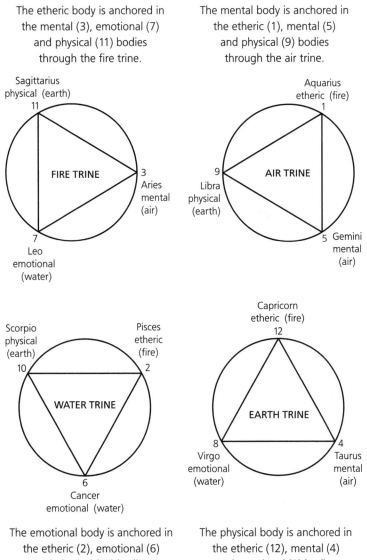

The etheric body is anchored in the mental (3), emotional (7) and physical (11) bodies through the fire trine.

The mental body is anchored in the etheric (1), mental (5) and physical (9) bodies through the air trine.

Sagittarius
physical (earth)
11

FIRE TRINE

3
Aries
mental
(air)

7
Leo
emotional
(water)

Aquarius
etheric (fire)
1

9
Libra
physical
(earth)

AIR TRINE

5 Gemini
mental
(air)

Scorpio
physical
(earth)
10

Pisces
etheric
(fire)
2

WATER TRINE

6
Cancer
emotional (water)

Capricorn
etheric (fire)
12

8
Virgo
emotional
(water)

EARTH TRINE

4
Taurus
mental
(air)

The emotional body is anchored in the etheric (2), emotional (6) and physical (10) bodies through the water trine.

The physical body is anchored in the etheric (12), mental (4) and emotional (8) bodies through the earth trine.

etheric, mental and physical bodies (but not the emotional body) anchor the mental body, thoughtforms that are living chalices, agents for the fiery Mind of God. The etheric, emotional and physical bodies (but not the mental body) anchor the emotional body to provide man with feeling and to break down the barriers of duality. Inasmuch as the mental body lacks the emotional tie and the emotional lacks the mental tie, their contact with each other is achieved through the etheric (mental contact with the emotional) or through the physical (emotional contact with the mental).

Patterns for the Distribution of Energy

The sending forth of energy from God to man is an activity of the masculine ray—of Spirit projecting the sacred fire into the planes of Matter for the purpose of the evolution of the soul in form. The distribution of this energy through the chakras begins with the anchoring of the threefold flame in the heart.

The heart is a prism through which the pure white light of Alpha and Omega energizes the four lower bodies according to their respective planes of consciousness. Within the heart, where the planes of Spirit and Matter converge, the threefold flame holds the balance of life.

Figure 11 illustrates the action of the threefold flame in a spiraling figure-eight pattern, ascending and descending from the throne of the heart. In the plane of Spirit above, the plumes are ascendant—the blue to one's left, the pink to one's right and the yellow in the center. In the plane of Matter below, the plumes are descendant—the blue on the right and the pink on the left, with the yellow remaining in the center.

The action of the flame above and below the heart determines the qualification of the energies that ascend and descend from the heart to the other six major chakras in the planes of

Spirit and Matter and thence to the seven subchakras and the remaining 130.

The cosmic energy that descends over the crystal cord is composed of two descending spirals, or stars. These stars are interlaced triangles of energy, one from Alpha having the plus spin, and one from Omega having the minus spin.

The Alpha star contains the fire (Alpha-plus) and air (Alpha-minus) triangles; the Omega star contains the water (Omega-minus) and earth (Omega-plus) triangles. These four triangles, carrying the frequencies of the four cosmic forces, seek their own plane and vibration in the chakras.

FIGURE 11: The threefold flame as a spiraling
figure-eight pattern uniting Spirit and Matter.

The Laws of Attraction and Polarity Govern Energy Flow

The law of attraction (likes attract) and the law of polarity (opposites polarize) are operative in the distribution and control of energy. The plane of Spirit (+) and the plane of Matter (–) are in polarity. Thus the three chakras above the heart are in polarity with the three chakras below the heart. (See figure 8, page 168.)

The throat, third-eye and crown chakras have a masculine or positive charge, and the solar-plexus, seat-of-the-soul and base-of-the-spine chakras have a feminine or negative charge. The heart, being the nexus between the planes of Matter and Spirit, has both positive and negative charges.

Now let us see how the law of attraction is operative in the distribution of energy through the upper and lower chakras, as the mist becomes the crystal in each of the chakras that govern the release of energy in their respective planes. The triangles of the Alpha and Omega spirals are distributed to the chakras through the ritual of creation, passing through the planes of fire, air, water and earth.

The fire and air triangles carry the energies of the vertical bar of the cross of precipitation (figure 12a). The interlacing of these triangles establishes the communion of the Monad with the fire of the One through the Mind of God.

The water and earth triangles carry the energies of the horizontal bar of the cross of precipitation (figure 12b). The interlacing of these triangles establishes the antahkarana for the community of the Holy Spirit, the One in action glorifying God through the Word and work of the Monad.

Aligned with the flow of energies through these four triangles, the Monad suspended in Matter can truly say, "I and my Father-Mother are one. My Father-Mother worketh hitherto, and I work."[10]

184

FIGURE 12: The cross of precipitation.

FIGURE 12A: The vertical bar of the cross of precipitation.

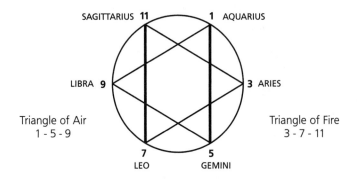

FIGURE 12B: The horizontal bar of the cross of precipitation.

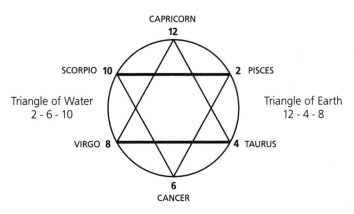

As God's energies descend into time and space, deterministic circular action-reaction patterns are converted into spiritually evolving spirals. This is brought about by the personhood of God, who through Self-identification transmutes the maya of duality even as it is created. Thus the soul who identifies with her Real Self can act through Christ as God's living presence, in the creation but not of it—that is, not defined by it (figure 13).

If we think of the Alpha-plus (fire-air) and Omega-minus (water-earth) stars descending via the crystal cord as trolley cars, and their triangles as four passengers that exit at four stops (at the heart chakra and the three chakras above and below), then we can understand how the energy is distributed in the four planes of Matter and in the four planes of Spirit according to the law of attraction.

The Spirit and Matter fire triangles exit at the heart. These carry the energies of the hierarchies of Aries, Leo and Sagittarius.

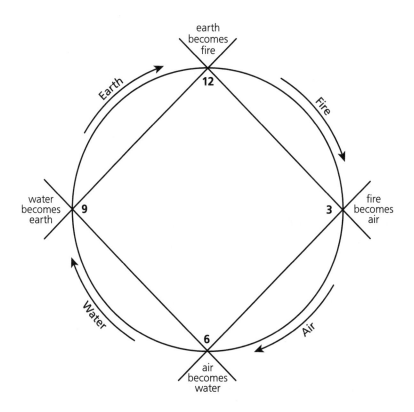

FIGURE 13: God in manifestation—the creation of spirals.
At the four cardinal points of transmutation there is a release of Christ-power through the divine alchemy. This power gives the impetus for rotation, or the creation of spirals, in the heart of the universe and in the heart of the atom.

The Spirit and Matter air triangles exit at the third eye and the seat of the soul. These carry the energies of the hierarchies of Aquarius, Gemini and Libra.

The Spirit and Matter water triangles exit at the throat and the solar plexus. These carry the energies of the hierarchies of Pisces, Cancer and Scorpio.

The Spirit and Matter earth triangles exit at the crown and the base of the spine. These carry the energies of the hierarchies of Capricorn, Taurus and Virgo.

Each time a triangle exits, the combined charges of the remaining triangles determine, by the law of attraction, where the next "stop" will be.

Let us examine the clockwise spiral that descends from the heart through the planes of Matter (figure 14a). When the Alpha-plus (fire) triangle exits in the heart (fire) chakra, three passengers are left: the Alpha-minus, the Omega-minus and the Omega-plus triangles.

Traveling as a unit in the trolley car, all proceed to the seat of the soul, impelled by the attraction between the Alpha-minus (air) triangle and the Alpha-minus charge of this (air) chakra. After the Alpha-minus triangle exits, the remaining passengers are the Omega-minus (water) and the Omega-plus (earth) triangles.

Functioning as a minus star, both are drawn to the "most minus" chakra, the solar plexus (water is more yin than earth).

At this Omega-minus (water) stop, the Omega-minus triangle exits. The last passenger, the Omega-plus triangle, is drawn to the base of the spine, the Omega-plus (earth) stop.

The identical process occurs above the heart over the ascending clockwise spiral for the distribution of energy through the planes of Spirit. The Alpha-minus triangle exits at the third-eye chakra, the Omega-minus triangle exits at the throat chakra and the Omega-plus triangle exits at the crown chakra.

The energy thus distributed is intended to be qualified

FIGURE 14: The distribution of energy in the chakras.

FIGURE 14A:	FIGURE 14B:	FIGURE 14C:
Clockwise distribution of energy from Spirit to Matter.	Caduceus action sustaining individuality.	Counterclockwise return of energy from Matter to Spirit.

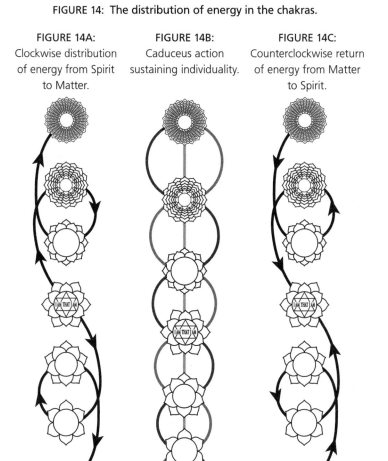

		Excess energy returns to the heart
		or
Materialization (clockwise spiral).	Sustainment of individuality through the figure-eight flow of energy over the caduceus.	individuality is lost through dematerialization of misqualified energy (counterclockwise spiral).

according to the seven rays, which correspond in frequency to the planes of Spirit and Matter focused through the seven chakras.

When there is no misqualification of energy through the chakras, only 10 percent of man's daily allotment is required to sustain his four lower bodies. Another 10 percent is destined to return through the heart chalice to the Source from whence it came, as a love tithing to the Almighty.

This flow of gratitude sustains the antahkarana between man and God, weaving the "stairway to the stars" that man will one day climb to his immortal freedom. The remaining 80 percent of man's daily allotment may be qualified with the highest creative intelligence and intent for the precipitation of the patterns made in the heavens through the patterns made in the earth in the seven chakras.

The Return of God's Energy to the Heart

By an act of Divine Will, the individual has the option to return to the heart chalice the energies that have been distributed to the upper and lower chakras in excess of their need for sustaining manifestation. The return of these energies occurs in the reverse order of their distribution (figure 14c).

Passing through the planes (chakras) of earth, water, air and fire, the triangles follow the pattern of the ritual of disintegration. This simply means that the triangles return to the heart, where they regroup in the Alpha-Omega star formations in readiness to be qualified through the prism of the Christ consciousness.

The purpose of returning one's surplus energies to the heart is to magnify the creative output of the soul by the combined energies (triangles) of the Alpha and Omega spirals through the momentum of the Christ anchored in the threefold flame, and through the sacred fire aspects of Spirit and Matter that are uniquely expressed in the heart. For in the heart the highest and noblest works of man are born. In the heart is the beginning of wisdom. In the heart the knowledge of love is given, and in the heart the might of the Spirit is felt and shared.

Man's option to return his excess energies to the heart chalice is elected by the authority of the God consciousness, the Christ consciousness, or the solar consciousness anchored in the third-eye, the heart, and the seat-of-the-soul chakras respectively. These decision-making faculties determine through the planes of fire and air how God's energies shall be used to create in Spirit and Matter.

The wisdom, love and power of the threefold flame are thus anchored in the mental body through (1) the third eye, the focus of the Divine Mind (yellow plume), which secures to man right knowledge and the singleness of vision and purpose of the All-Seeing Eye of God; (2) the heart (pink plume), which releases the intuitive knowledge of the Christ Self; and (3) the seat of the soul (blue plume), which impresses the outer mind with the determination of the soul to bring forth the divine plan according to its fiery destiny.

The consciousness of duality opposes these faculties of heart, head and hand through (1) the human intellect, which proclaims the wisdom of the world as superior to the wisdom of God; (2) the human ego, which usurps the authority of the Christ; and (3) the human will, which flaunts the Divine Will and the laws of God, justifying by man-made codes its unbridled use of God's energy.

When God's energies are invested in duality, they become cloaked in maya. The resurrection and the life of Christ is absent from their wayward meandering. But all energy that has come forth from the Godhead via the circle of spiral (through the distribution of energies described above) must return to him via the figure-eight pattern of the caduceus. For every descending cycle, there should be an ascending figure eight.

When these patterns are not worthy of being perpetuated (immortalized), then the energy that has come forth over the clockwise spiral returns to Spirit via the counterclockwise spiral. This process, known as dematerialization, is used to strip the energy of the imperfect patterns and to remove the stamp of individuality.

The energy that passes from Matter to Spirit via the counterclockwise spiral is thus returned by the process of repolarization to the reservoir of God's power, to be used again in the perfect creations of God and man.

My Heart Is the Heart of God

The heart chalice provides the greatest potential for balanced precipitation in the planes of Spirit and Matter because it is the focus of the sacred fire—the threefold flame. Here the union of Spirit-fire and Matter-fire, focusing the power of the masculine and feminine polarity of the Godhead, produces in man the full-orbed radiance of the Christ consciousness.

As the pivot point between the upper and lower chakras, the heart chalice receives on the return cycle the perfectly balanced energies of Spirit-earth/Matter-earth, of Spirit-water/Matter-water, and of Spirit-air/Matter-air. These energies are refined by the celestial fires of the heart, molded by the quickening action of the threefold flame, and released through the prism of the Christ consciousness for the blessing of all life.

Through the crystal cord (the lifeline of the Presence), the heart of man is connected directly to the heart of God. When properly attuned with the trinity of the Creator's consciousness, man becomes a co-creator with him, his heartbeat one with the pulsation of the divine heartbeat, his mind flowing with the creative intent, his soul humming with the rhythm of the spheres.

How Man Limits the Threefold Flame

The threefold flame can never be contaminated by the abuses of men. But when man fails to adore it, its size may be significantly reduced. When man fails to invoke it in balanced action, its three plumes may assume different heights. Or when man fails to purify his thoughts and feelings, motives and intent, the threefold flame may become buried in astral debris. But the flame itself burns on to sustain life in the four lower bodies until the crystal cord is withdrawn by the Holy Christ Self and opportunity recedes until another round.

The purification of the heart chakra and the balancing of the threefold flame are essential if man is to become a co-creator with God. The threefold flame must be cultivated and nourished through prayer, meditation and decrees, and through service to life.

If man would progress spiritually, he must invoke the sacred fire to remove the debris that accumulates around the heart chakra—and until he does, his evolution is at a standstill. The heart must be bathed daily in violet fire, blue lightning and the flame of the Holy Spirit if he is to expand and balance the threefold flame and free himself from the bondage of the senses that enslave the heart. Truly, he whose heart remains buried in a tomb of matter is himself not quickened from the dead.

It has been said, "As [a man] thinketh in his heart, so is he."[11] The heart is the fount of man's being. Therefore, if the motive of the heart is pure, man's energies will flow from the heart in a pure stream and return to him in like manner. If the motive of the heart is impure, the energies that flow from the heart and the other chakras will likewise be impure.

The pure in heart see God[12] because there is an unbroken stream of light that flows from the pure heart to the heart of the one Source of all life. The strength of Galahad was as the strength of ten because the magnification of the full potential of the Christ was possible through his pure heart flame. To become God-realized, man must guard the heart, adore the flame, and purify his consciousness. Then he will be able to say with Jesus:

> My heart is the heart of God.
> My heart is the heart of the world.
> My heart is the heart of Christ in healing action.

The Caduceus

Having examined the descent of the Alpha and Omega energies and the pattern of their distribution in man, let us now turn to the action of the caduceus, the figure-eight spirals over which God's energy ascends through the planes of Matter and Spirit from the seed atom in the base of the spine to the lodestone of the Presence in the crown for the sustainment of individuality (figure 14b).

Only through a proper understanding of the caduceus can the mastery of life's sacred energies be successfully accomplished. For only in the victory of the caduceus can man vanquish the last enemy, which is death.

The descent of energy from God to man, being a masculine activity of the sacred fire, infuses the chakras with the masculine (positive) charge. The ascent of the sacred fire from man to God via the caduceus, being a feminine activity, infuses the chakras with the feminine (negative) charge of the Godhead. Through our study of the caduceus we shall see how these dual functions combine to produce the Christ consciousness in the planes of Spirit and Matter.

The winged staff, symbol of the medical profession, illustrates the entwining of the masculine (blue) and feminine (pink) rays in a centripetal and centrifugal action around the rod of the Christ (yellow) focused in the spinal column.

The energies of the seed atom rise from the base of the spine to the crown chakra in a triune action of the sacred fire corresponding to the threefold flame. These energies are called in Sanskrit the *pingala* (corresponding to the blue plume), the *sushumna* (corresponding to the yellow plume), and the *ida* (corresponding to the pink plume). Theosophist C. W. Leadbeater says, "In a man the *Idā* starts from the base of the spine just on the left of the *Sushumnā* and the *Pingalā* on the right (be it understood that I mean the right and left of the *man,* not the spectator); but in a woman these positions are reversed."[13] (See figure 15.)

The threefold caduceus spiral that rises on the spinal ladder has its source in the white fire core of the seed atom and in the focus of the microcosmic Causal Body surrounding it. This focus of the World Mother and of the action of the feminine ray in man magnetizes the energies of the Holy Spirit, which are active to a greater or lesser degree in all.

Beginning at the base of the spine, the *ida* and *pingala* (corresponding to the sympathetic nervous system) weave a figure-eight pattern, meeting the *sushumna* (corresponding to the central nervous system) at each of the seven centers.

The *pingala* is the Omega-plus triangle, representing the earth element; the *ida* is the Omega-minus triangle, representing the water element; while the *sushumna* is the Alpha star containing the descending Alpha-plus triangle (fire) and the ascending Alpha-minus triangle (air).

One's individual mastery in the planes of fire, air, water and earth determines the intensity of color and flow in the energies of the *ida, pingala* and *sushumna.* Just as the threefold flame may be imbalanced according to the level of one's attainment, so the members of the caduceus are not necessarily equal.

In the unawakened lifestream, only the energies of the

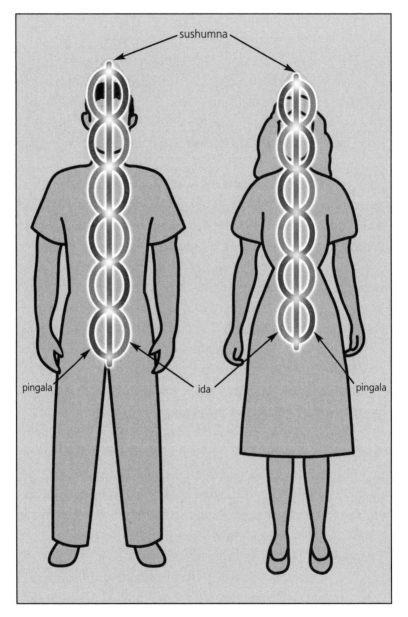

FIGURE 15: The caduceus.
The light-energy-consciousness of the Divine Mother rising upon
the spine as the caduceus in a figure-eight flow. The *pingala* (blue),
the *sushumna* (yellow) and the *ida* (pink) intertwine and
converge at each of the seven major chakras.

outer sphere (the blue band) of the microcosmic Causal Body are active in producing the caduceus spirals; the fires of the seed atom remain dormant, sealed within the white fire core. Nevertheless, the energies of the outer sphere are sufficient to sustain the flow of the *ida, pingala* and *sushumna* from the base of the spine to the crown.

Thus, man is never without the flow of the feminine ray rising upon the spinal altar, even as he is never without the descending currents of the masculine ray posited in the three-fold flame within the heart.

Let it be clear, then, that the descending cycles of the Alpha-Omega currents within the being of man come forth from the Father aspect, focused in the individualized I AM Presence and in the lodestone of the Presence, which is located in the crown chakra. The ascending cycles of the Alpha-Omega currents come forth from the Mother aspect of the Deity, focused through the seed atom and the microcosmic Causal Body surrounding it at the base-of-the-spine chakra.

In this manner the promise is fulfilled that was given to David: "The LORD shall preserve thy going out and thy coming in from this time forth, and even for evermore."[14] The inner meaning of the promise is that the LORD shall preserve the going out of his sacred energies from the Holy of Holies—the I AM Presence—into the body temple through the masculine and feminine rays, and he will also preserve their safe return to the Causal Body by the power of the Christ light released through the chakras.

This mystery was revealed to Jacob in a dream: "And behold a ladder [the spinal ladder] set up on the earth [upon the base-of-the-spine chakra, the plane of Matter-earth], and the top of it reached to heaven [to the crown chakra, the plane of Spirit-earth]: and behold the angels of God ascending and descending on it."[15]

Here the term "angels" symbolizes the particles of energy (electrons)—or triangles as we have shown them—that move in a continuous flow up and down the spine.

Figure 14 (page 187) summarizes the flow of God's energy in man. The energies of the I AM Presence descend from Spirit to Matter via the clockwise spiral (figure 14a). Energy flows from the heart to the base-of-the-spine chakra through Matter-fire (heart), Matter-air (seat of the soul), Matter-water (solar plexus) and Matter-earth (base of the spine). It flows from the heart to the crown chakra through Spirit-fire (heart), Spirit-air (third eye), Spirit-water (throat) and Spirit-earth (crown). This is represented on the Cosmic Clock as a circle in the clockwise direction.

Correctly qualified energies, which sustain individuality in the world of form, travel up and down the spine via the figure-eight flow of the caduceus (figure 14b). Energy flowing from the base-of-the-spine chakra to the heart is represented on the Cosmic Clock as a counterclockwise figure-eight pattern. The energy flows through Matter-earth (base of the spine), Matter-air (seat of the soul), Matter-water (solar plexus) and Matter-fire (heart). The energy continuing on from the heart to the crown chakra is represented on the Cosmic Clock as a clockwise figure-eight pattern. It flows through Spirit-fire (heart), Spirit-water (throat), Spirit-air (third eye) and Spirit-earth (crown).

Excess energies as well as redeemed misqualified energies return to the heart via the counterclockwise spiral (figure 14c). Energy flows from the base-of-the-spine chakra to the heart through Matter-earth (base of the spine), Matter-water (solar plexus), Matter-air (seat of the soul) and Matter-fire (heart). It flows from the crown chakra to the heart through Spirit-earth (crown), Spirit-water (throat), Spirit-air (third eye) and Spirit-fire (heart). This is represented on the Cosmic Clock as a circle in the counterclockwise direction.

The Spinal Altar

As the focal point for the flow of the sacred fire in man, the spine is the axis of creation. It has been called the rod of Meru, or *merudanda,* and appropriately so. For the God and Goddess Meru hold the focus of the feminine ray for the earth. The spine, as the focal point for the precipitation of the four lower bodies, represents the Mother or Matter side of creation.

Our examination of a cross section of the spine at the etheric level reveals three rings—another action of the Trinity—that are actually canals for the flow of the sacred fire. The center canal (blue), called the *chitrini,* is the passageway for the raising of the seed atom. The next ring (pink), called the *vajrini,* is the passageway for the distribution of energies from the I AM Presence through the heart to the chakras. The outermost ring (yellow), the *sushumna,* is the passageway for the yellow flame of the caduceus (figure 16).

The seven chakras are connected to one another, to the seven main subchakras and to the remaining 130 chakras by etheric tubes called *nadis. Nadi* is the Sanskrit word for "tube, vessel or vein," derived from the root word *nad* meaning

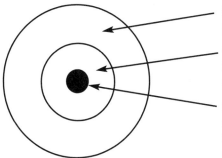

Sushumna—energy of the yellow flame of the caduceus.

Vajrini—energy distributed from the heart through the pink canal.

Chitrini—seed atom (white) rises up the blue canal. Chakras are tied to the blue canal.

FIGURE 16: The central channel of the caduceus.

"motion," suggesting the concept of energy flowing through the body.

These *nadis* are actually forcefields that direct the currents to their proper levels, carrying the energies of the sacred fire to and from the heart chalice. Over these same etheric pathways, the threefold energies of the caduceus ascend the spinal ladder.

Interlaced Triangles

The Trinity of the Mother Ray (the rising caduceus) and the energies of the Father Ray (the descending spirals of the crystal cord) converge at the seven chakras. The fusion of their patterns infuses the four lower bodies with the balance of divine polarity, and there is an accompanying release of the Christ light.

The converging of the masculine and feminine rays in the chakras is seen as the rising triangle (feminine) meets the descending triangle (masculine). As the two triangles interlace over each succeeding chakra, the star of man's divinity is born, duality is transcended, and there is a return to the whole-eye consciousness of the Godhead (figure 17).

Man is never more complete than when the energies of the Father-Mother God merge in the seven purified chalices of his being. For then the image of the Christ is released through the chakras in the planes of fire, air, water and earth.

This unique manifestation of the Christ flame within the chakras qualifies man's energy with the polarity necessary for its return to the Causal Body. That which returns to the secret place of the Most High, the place of perfection, must be perfected according to the divine polarity realized in the consciousness of the Christ.

In order to qualify for immortality, man must be found in the likeness of the Father-Mother God. Likewise, the energies

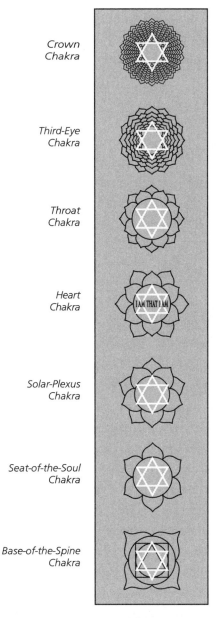

Crown
Chakra

Third-Eye
Chakra

Throat
Chakra

Heart
Chakra

I AM THAT I AM

Solar-Plexus
Chakra

Seat-of-the-Soul
Chakra

Base-of-the-Spine
Chakra

FIGURE 17:
The merging of Father-Mother God
brings forth the Christ at each level of being.

and the creations he sends forth from the seven planes of his being must be stamped with the Christ consciousness, which is produced from the interlaced masculine and feminine rays within the seven chakras.

The law of polarity operative in the being of man is both exact and exacting. Unless he maintains a balanced flow of the yin and yang energies in his four lower bodies, man leaves himself open to disease, decay, unhappiness, and the symptoms of old age. Moreover, he is incapable of drawing and holding abundant supply to meet his spiritual and material needs. These signs of incompleteness are the result of man's inability to maintain the balance of the Father-Mother God in his thoughts, feelings, words and actions.

Expressing Inner Perfection

The natural state of man is wholeness. The return to that state cannot be accomplished as long as man misqualifies the energies that descend from his I AM Presence. For in so doing he is not able to sustain the action of the masculine ray within the chakras that is necessary to magnetize the feminine ray, thereby accelerating the action of the caduceus.

When the entire process of perfectionment is wholeheartedly pursued, the powerful currents of the masculine ray flowing through the chakras, qualified by the Christly virtues of the seven rays, magnetize an equally powerful action of the feminine ray from the seed atom.

As the initiate attains greater mastery in the qualification of light through the chakras, the seven spheres of the microcosmic Causal Body surrounding the seed atom gradually "unwind," releasing the energies of the feminine ray that intensify the action of the caduceus.

Then at the hour of transfiguration (which occurs when

man has mastered the seven planes of consciousness through the proper qualification of the energies released from the I AM Presence), the seed atom (Kundalini) emerges from the white fire core and the initiate shines like the sun, even as Jesus did (figure 18).[16]

Rising up the *chitrini,* it infuses each of the seven chakras with the solar consciousness of the lifestream—the feminine action of the Christ—and with the pattern of its fiery destiny released from within the white fire core of the microcosmic Causal Body.

As the seed atom rises, man becomes literally a blazing sun. For the divine union of the Father-Mother God that is fulfilled within each chalice produces therein the immaculate conception of the Christ.

FIGURE 18: The union of God and man through the transfiguration.

When the divine polarity is thus attained in each of the seven planes of his consciousness and the seed atom is anchored in the lodestone of the I AM Presence, the perfect balance of man's androgynous nature is realized in Spirit and in Matter.

Having passed this initiation, man is given unlimited power to create in the planes of Spirit and Matter[17] according to the unique designs—the patterns made in the heavens—held within his own individualized Causal Body.

Speaking of the mystical union of the life fires in man, beloved Amaryllis says: "When the anointing of the Holy Spirit descends upon the planetary body, it first descends upon the human heart. Then there occurs a natural opening of the spiritual centers in man, and at that moment the kingdom of God first begins to blush into reality as a rising sun of hope[18] that gladdens hearts who have watched through the long night of pain and struggle.

"Now they behold the beauty of God, and all whose centers are thus opened rush into the orchestra of cosmic grace to participate in the creation of that beautiful music that gladdens heart and soul, that brings delight to every child and child-man. And so when the centers open naturally in man, God's kingdom becomes a shared kingdom."[19]

When the threefold flame is balanced and the four lower bodies are in alignment according to the pattern of the square within the circle, the crystal chalices function at maximum efficiency as catalysts for the fulfillment in man of the law of correspondences. The mandate "As Above, so below" is realized as the positive spirals of Christly virtue, emanating from each of the 144 centers, produce one giant clockwise spiral that begins in the heart and culminates in the lodestone of the I AM Presence.

The weaving of the deathless solar body is the action of

this giant spiral, which students on the Path may visualize and drawn forth, although the spiral is not sustained in unascended man until he has passed the initiation of the transfiguration.

The Goddess Kundalini

Various yogic systems teach different methods for raising the seed atom, or Kundalini. It is considered the supreme goal of yoga to achieve the awakening of the inner layers of the Kundalini fires and then the raising of the Kundalini, through meditation, exercise and various practices.

It is said that the union of the soul with God is accomplished when the Goddess Kundalini is awakened by psychic heat induced by yogic practices, in the same manner as a serpent struck by a rod hisses and straightens itself. Until this is accomplished, the Goddess Kundalini lies sleeping in the root chakra coiled like a serpent three-and-a-half times at the base, her head blocking the opening of the *sushumna* canal.

The yogins teach that the goal of the Goddess Kundalini is to unite with her Lord Shiva in the crown chakra. They explain that as she proceeds up the *chitrini* canal, she pierces the chakras with her lightning energies, the flowers turn upward, and the flow of life through the chakras is greatly enhanced.

Kundalini draws into herself (into latency) the psychological functions (the characteristics of the Christ consciousness) of each chakra. She then continues on to fulfill the goal of ultimate reunion—the mystical oneness of Shakti (the Mother-Goddess—feminine aspect of the Cosmic Mind) with Shakta (the Father-God—masculine aspect of the Cosmic Mind). This results in enlightenment—the unfolding of the thousand-petaled lotus, whereby man realizes his God consciousness.

Once this state is attained, Kundalini descends the *chitrini,* entering each chakra and giving back to it the functions that she absorbed during the ascent, charged with the energies she has received from her Lord.

Some yogic masters teach their disciples to retain the Kundalini in the heart chakra to lend greater momentum to the release of light from this center, while others teach them to conclude their meditation by leading Kundalini back to the base chakra.

It takes many years for the disciple—who usually goes into a partial trance while raising the Kundalini—to raise the Kundalini from the base to the crown chakra. Using the force of his will, he may raise it a little higher with each meditation. An adept is capable of raising the Kundalini from the base to the crown chakra in the space of an hour.

During their meditations on the Kundalini, these devotees send out to the world through the seven planes of consciousness the concentrated power of the Christ that is activated as the Kundalini enters each chakra.

These and other meditations of the true unascended masters of the Himalayas have served for thousands of years to provide the open door for the light to flow into a darkened world, and to raise mankind's consciousness and sustain it at levels beyond that which the unenlightened masses could reach on their own.

Regarding the concept of Kundalini, the Ascended Masters have given us the term "seed atom" because it signifies the focusing within the planes of Matter, within the Mother consciousness, of the full potential of that which is destined to be realized in the plane of Spirit, in the Father consciousness, through the alchemical marriage—the union of Matter and Spirit.

The pattern of the whole of the microcosm—here defined as the material universe—is focused within the seed atom as the negative aspect of divine power. The pattern of the whole of the Macrocosm—the spiritual universe—is focused within the lodestone of the I AM Presence as the positive aspect of divine power.

Thus when the seed atom is raised, the personality of man merges with the impersonality of God. In merging with the ocean, the drop is not lost, however. It gains permanent Self-realization as the Impersonal Impersonality (the Father), the Impersonal Personality (the Son), the Personal Personality (the Mother) and the Personal Impersonality (the Holy Spirit) of the Godhead. Truly the goal of yoga, the union of you and God, is the transmutation of the limited human self into the unlimited Divine Self.

When this transformation occurs, the adept not only focuses in the earth the radiant energies of his personal victory, but he also becomes an outpost of the Great White Brotherhood who can effect great change for God's purposes in the earth. Mother Mary speaks of the tremendous gift that each one who raises the Mother light gives to God: "The raising of the fires of the Goddess Kundalini is ultimately for the release of the light of the crown and for the vision of the third eye. The track over which this energy flows is like a shepherd's crook, coming up the spine and over the head. And so you see, when you raise the energy of Mother, you become a staff in the hand of the Lord. You become the staff of Moses, the staff of Christ—those who uphold the flame of the hierarchs of the age."[20]

Dangers Involved in Raising the Kundalini

Because of the intense powers of the Kundalini, which overnight may make men spiritual giants or demons, it is not advisable to seek to raise the Kundalini unless one is under the guidance and protection of a true unascended master. The Ascended Masters recommend that students meditate only upon the chakras in the plane of Spirit—those above and including the heart chalice.

Visualizing the raising of a white-fire ball from the level of the heart to the I AM Presence is the safest meditation for the raising of the seed atom. It simulates in the plane of Spirit the raising of the Kundalini, without any danger of actually arousing the Kundalini fires until the lifestream has drawn such a momentum of power in the upper chakras and in the lodestone of the I AM Presence as to counterbalance any remaining untransmuted substance that may be aroused as the Kundalini rises through the planes of Matter.

If the Ascended Master student uses this meditation to focus the consciousness of the Christ in the planes of Spirit-fire, Spirit-water, Spirit-air and Spirit-earth, visualizing the white-fire ball rising through the heart, throat, third-eye and crown chakras en route to the Christ Self and the I AM Presence, he will never need to meditate upon the chakras below the heart, for they will automatically be purified through their connection to the four cosmic forces.

Nevertheless, the student may visualize the action of the violet flame and other aspects of the sacred fire swirling through his entire being as shown on the lower figure of the Chart of Your Divine Self (facing page 74).

There is never any possibility of the student misusing the fires of creation if the seed atom is raised according to the initiatic timetable—that is, if the initiations of the sacred fire preparatory to and preceding the raising of the seed atom are successfully passed. Then the release of God-power, God-wisdom and God-love through the being of man can only intensify the good that the lifestream has already outpictured.

But there is indeed grave danger to the lifestream if the raising of the Kundalini is forced prior to (1) the invocation of the sacred fire for the transmutation of impurities in the four lower bodies and electronic belt; (2) the clearing of the astral debris that accumulates at the vortices of light—at the chakras; (3) the balancing of the threefold flame; and (4) the alignment of the four lower bodies and the manifestation of God-dominion over the human intellect, ego and will.

The Kundalini fires animate whatever is present in the world of man as they ascend the spinal altar. If the passions of the flesh and the temptations of the world still have hold upon his consciousness, these, together with his human creation, may be magnified by the Kundalini to the point of unhinging his mind. When the sex drive is amplified by the Kundalini, it may rage in his being as an uncontrollable force, causing him to behave as a wild beast and ultimately to become insane.

The dangers involved in playing with the Kundalini fires cannot be overstated. We have seen the tragic results of the rape of the Divine Mother and the abuse of the sacred path of the Kundalini by the violent who have sought to take heaven (the crown chakra) by force (by forcing the raising of the Kundalini).

We have seen that the tearing of the garment of the soul and the burning of the solar faculties that has resulted from such madness has affected lifestreams for numerous embodiments following their indiscretion.

Wise, therefore, is the student who heeds this warning. Placing his hand in the hand of his own Christ Self, he is content to walk the Path under the direction of his God Presence in the calm and certain knowing that if he does all things well, fulfilling the precepts of the Law in service and in grace, he will attain the supreme goal of reunion based on self-mastery.[21]

The Mastery of Energy in the Seven Planes

The Ascended Masters have shown us that it is altogether possible for the advanced student to raise the seed atom prior to the transfiguration. If this should occur, it is highly unlikely that the seed atom will remain in the crown chakra. It may descend to the heart chalice to magnify the power of the Christ in the planes of Spirit-fire and Matter-fire, or it may well return to the base of the spine.

If sufficient mastery over the seven planes and the release of the seven rays through the seven chakras is attained prior to raising the seed atom, the energies within the chakras will be in perfect polarity. Then when the seed atom enters each chakra, it will absorb the feminine aspect of the Christ already anchored there.

Drawing a greater and greater momentum of the feminine ray as it rises, the seed atom has a greater forcefield of attraction to the lodestone, which simultaneously magnetizes to itself the masculine aspect of the Christ focused in the chakras. In this manner, during the raising of the seed atom all of the energies of man are polarized to the planes of Spirit-earth and Matter-earth.

The chakras are the focus of the Christ, of the masculine and feminine rays in man (in *man*ifestation)—and the seed atom and lodestone are the focuses of the Father-Mother God. Thus the Divine Mother draws into herself the feminine aspect of man from within the chakras, and the Divine Father draws into himself the masculine aspect of man from within the chakras.

As long as the union of Matter and Spirit is sustained— that is, while the seed atom remains in the lodestone—man will be able to remain in nirvana or samadhi. In this state, his consciousness is withdrawn from all planes except Spirit-earth and Matter-earth.

This gives him a direct tie to the planes of Spirit-earth and Matter-earth in the Causal Body—the first and second spheres of purity and illumination, which are the open doors to the spheres of the five secret rays held between them, the planes of nirvana.

When the seed atom returns either to the heart or to the base-of-the-spine chakra, the action of the masculine and feminine rays in man is returned to the chakras that the God consciousness has accelerated.

When all other conditions necessary for the transfiguration have been met, the raising of the seed atom and its union with the lodestone—which takes place during this initiation—produces in the four lower bodies the transfiguring power of the Holy Spirit, whereby man becomes God and God becomes man.

Once the initiation of the transfiguration is passed, the seed atom may descend the "Mount of Transfiguration," but it never again descends lower than the heart chalice. For man has transcended the planes of Matter and his spirit no longer dwells in those planes.

Higher and Ever Higher

In the initiation of the resurrection, the seed atom is permanently anchored in the lodestone. The action of the Christ in the plane of Spirit-fire and Matter-fire (in the heart chakra) comes into perfect polarity with the action of the Father-Mother God, where the plane of Spirit-earth and Matter-earth have united (in the crown chakra).

In the initiation of the ascension, the focus of the Father-Mother God anchored in the lodestone and the seed atom descends to the heart chalice. There the full potential of the Godhead merges with the full potential of the Christ. God in Christ then affirms the victory of the I AM Presence in the planes of Spirit and Matter ("I AM a blazing sun!") and the microcosm ascends into the Macrocosm. Elisha witnessed this tremendous release of light when he saw his guru, Elijah, ascend in a chariot of fire.[22]

Mother Mary says we do not need to wait for our ascension, as the fingers of God reach out to touch those who would attune to their victory here and now: "The sound of far-off worlds is heard in the hearts of the lonely ones, and they are lonely no longer. The collapse of the universe into the microcosm of man is the surrender of the Eternal One to the individual. The flame caresses the soul. And as God draws nigh within the flame, understanding is born and all of the pieces of the strange puzzle of life rise into place as a cosmic picture of celestial hope."[23]

Now the being of man (as the rising triangle) merges with the being of God (the descending triangle), and man becomes one with the star that once shone over the place where the infant Christ was born. The heart of man becomes one with the heart of God.

The ascension is the victory of the law of cycles. God in man is omnipotent, omniscient and omnipresent. Man in God is all-powerful, all-knowing and everywhere in the Presence of the LORD.

The Crystal of Purity

The mastery of self through the mastery of life's energies is summed up in one word: purity. Indeed, those who have ascended before us avow that their victory was born out of purity of thought, word and deed—and out of their fastidious attention to the purification of their four lower bodies and their chalices.

From time to time, disciples on the path have been privileged to receive admonishment from the Goddess of Purity. Her counsel is born out of her devotion to the flame of purity, which has lifted many a soul out of the degradation of astral confusion into the light of her native solar consciousness. From the Goddess of Purity's retreat in Madagascar and her focus of healing have come inspiration and hope for the dawn of the Age of Enlightenment.

Simply she has said, "Purity, beloved ones, begins with a single crystal, the crystal of your consciousness. And from the point of the flame within the center of the crystal begins the expansion of the consciousness of purity. The pure in heart see God through the crystal of their own consciousness, which they have made God's consciousness.

"When you have mastered the many facets of the single crystal, then other crystals will be added unto you with many more facets of opportunity for self-mastery. And so, you see, each crystal denotes another step of initiation to the brothers and sisters serving in my retreat here in Madagascar.

"In our beautiful island in the sea we have consecrated our energies to the crystal diadem of purity that is the consciousness of God, and as the flame passes through the crystal—the mingling of the mist and the crystal, of the formed and the unformed—there is a release of the Cosmic Christ consciousness to the earth."

In the same discourse she gently reminded the students to keep the crystal of their consciousness pure: "Those who truly love will keep the crystal polished so that all of the myriad hues of the diamond-shining Mind of God will be reflected throughout their consciousness.

"Smudges appear easily on the crystal as one moves through the outer world that has been polluted by mankind's consciousness. Carefully one must take from one's pocket the velvet cloth to polish the crystal.

"Keep it clean as though it were the very dearest object of your affection, for at the moment when the virgins (the holy Ascended Lady Masters) come to infuse you with the momentum of their purity and the seraphim gather, having come lately from the very throne of God himself to bring to you a drop of purity from his heart—at that moment, precious ones, the crystal must be polished, else it cannot reflect the flame within the drop of purity.

"But if the crystal be polished, then the flame within the drop, taken from the ocean of God's flaming purity, can merge with the flame that is in the center of your crystal. A fiery magnetic attraction impels the purity of God to the center of each flaming crystal.

"But when there is darkness surrounding the crystal—between the flame within and the flame without—then penetration cannot occur. Blessed are the pure in heart, for they shall indeed see the consciousness of God's flaming purity."

The Goddess of Purity then announced that she and her angels bore gifts for all who were prepared to receive them: "I come this day bearing many crystals, and so do my angels. They are spherical crystals, beloved ones, and they are to be placed over those chakras in each one of you and in each one upon the planetary body who is ready to receive the stepping-up of the release of the flame through the seven centers anchored in the four lower bodies of man.

"Each of the crystals that we bear is designated for a specific chakra of a specific individual. God has individualized himself in these crystals that I carry. And after the pattern of each one's own flaming identity, he has fashioned the crystal that is designed to unlock your divine blueprint through each of the seven chakras.

"Not everyone will receive a crystal for each chakra, and there are some in the world who are qualified to receive several more than some of you here. For God is no respecter of the human personality. He looks at the Law of thy being, of each one's being. He calculates. He draws up the fires of initiations passed, of light released, and the cosmic computer releases the exact judgment for each lifestream.

"Therefore, as you have sown, so shall you reap.[24] And if you feel that you would like additional crystals in time to come, then remember that the development of the light, the service to the seven rays and to the diamond-shining Mind of God will ensure to you the mastery of the four lower bodies and of the four elements that must precede the opening of the chakras.

"My angels stand in position over you and over the students of light throughout the world, and they are now placing the crystals over the chakras in each one of you."

This dispensation from the Lords of Karma presents a challenge to all who seek the prize of purity, for the Goddess of Purity has said that all who read this dictation and diligently prepare their consciousness may likewise receive the gift of the crystals.

"Beloved ones, the crystal will magnify the light or the darkness that is in you. 'If therefore the light that is in thee be darkness, how great is that darkness!' "[25]

Later she explained to us that the crystals placed over the chakras would function as transformers to accelerate both the release of light from the chakras and the transmutation of the remaining human consciousness surrounding the chakras. She also warned the students of the urgency of the times:

"You are at the point of no return. You must therefore surrender the darkness, that the darkness might become light. For when you surrender the darkness into the flame, the flame consumes the night and returns to you the light. And that light is a fire that travels the spiral of the crystal and releases the outburst of the sparks of purity through each of your chakras that is covered with the crystal."

In conclusion, she gave welcome advice and instruction on the handling of misqualified energy and the ritual of bathing the chakras:

"Precious ones, do not struggle with the untransmuted energies that accumulate around the chakras. For each chakra is a mighty sun, a whirling sun that is a vortex of light drawing into itself for transmutation all human creation and releasing simultaneously the light from the heart of the I AM Presence. Therefore, you must expect that untransmuted energy will collect at the brightest chakras, for there it has the greatest possibility of finding release.

"As the ancients performed daily ablutions in holy water, so may I remind you to perform daily the sacrament of bathing the chakras, of releasing into the flame the energies that gather there for transmutation, so that the full-orbed manifestation of the light of God can blaze through the crystals we have placed over the chakras.

"Won't you train yourself upon awakening, after you have made your initial invocations to the flame of the Almighty One, to call for this transmutation, for the fiery essence of the sacred fire breath to go forth and to draw off all accumulations of negativity around the seven chakras?

"This simple exercise is practiced by the brothers and sisters in our retreat, for I have shown them that such practice will insure a swift momentum, a swift rising of their light into the light.

"The light in you must become one with the light in the heart of the Universal, in the heart of the God Presence. To that end do we maintain our focus of purity. To that end have we come this day—that the light may become one with the light, that the flame may return to the home of the flame, that all may come full circle, that you may experience the resurrection during the cycles of the return of karma, which ought to be cycles of transmutation.

"These cycles are stepped up for the elect, beloved ones. Fear not, then, when your karma appears as a mighty legion upon the horizon, as a mighty army that comes forth to defeat the Christ. Fear not, but stand with the prophet upon the hillside. Raise your right hand as the authority of your I AM Presence and say to your own human creation: 'I refuse to accept your domination any longer! Go down before the sun of the Almighty! Go down before the flame of the Most High God!'

"Stand thus before the Goliath of your own human consciousness, beloved ones, and fear not, retreat not. Draw courage from the love of purity, draw courage from the crystal, draw courage from the flame in the center of the crystal."

Then, smiling a smile of loveliness, the Goddess of Purity said: "Do you feel all buttoned up with crystals? Well, then, remember that the buttons that shall appear upon the seamless garment of your divinity are the crystals upon the seven chakras.

"I pray that you will make use of those that have been given unto you, that in due course you might all receive the full complement of crystals reflecting the seven rays and the focus of the crystal diadem in our retreat.

"My purity I leave with you. My focus is already here. Through it I pour to you each day a greater awareness and consciousness of the purity of your mission, of your divine plan, of the seven color rays and their meaning in your life.

"Seek purity and find it, for it will illumine the entire Law of thy being.

> "In the victory of purity I came.
> In victory's flame I came—
> To victory's flame I return.
> In the oneness of his love I remain,
> And I AM the Goddess of Purity."[26]

Chapter 7

The One Path above the Many: Mysticism

*To give perfect expression to the One, the
Infinite, through the harmony of the many...
is the object alike of our individual life
and our society.*

RABINDRANATH TAGORE

The One Path
above the Many:
Mysticism

ONE OF THE UNFORTUNATE tactics of the negative powers on the planet is the continual misdirection of mankind's consciousness into states of criticism, condemnation and judgment. This includes criticizing the doctrines or supposed tenets of various faiths. Often individuals passing judgment on an individual or a religion are not aware of just what people think or mean by what they print or say.

For example, in the name of spiritual progress, the Masters of Wisdom release an idea through one or more spiritual organizations. Other individuals may say, by their misinterpretation of this release, "They think they are the only ones." The result of such criticism is that the intended good cannot flow into their world. Their remark closes the door against Truth, not only for themselves but for others who come under their sphere of influence.

Nothing can so effectively stop people from receiving their victory as criticizing the faith of others. Nothing constructive is ever achieved by degrading or tearing down any religious faith.

Yet the standards and conduct of many religious faiths have produced scurrilous effects.

This criticism comes about because man humanizes the Deity. Making a God in his own image, he justifies all types of mortal thought and feeling that are contrary to what Jesus or any of the great Masters would entertain.

"Divide and conquer" is a method the negative forces use successfully. Man's propensity to condemn has for thousands of years kept him under the tyranny of negative patterns. In fact, individuals who do the same things they criticize are often the most violent in their condemnation of others. And some individuals who think that others do the same things as they do will condemn them for it whether they know it to be true or not.

The Path That Leads to God-Realization

We must recognize that all of this is a deterrent intended to keep man from finding the one Path that leads to God-realization. Some organizations are more progressive, while others are more reactionary and stultified. But there is a thread of continuity running through all true religions that allows the sincere seeker to find some element of good in them, if he has the good within himself or at least the potential to acknowledge it.

"The best things in life are free" is a commonly accepted statement. But in reality, the best things in life, because they are the most magnificent, will prove the most costly in hours of devotion, sacrifice, attention, effort and will.

Some religious faiths throughout the world feel that they will successfully perpetuate their own brand of theology, retain their membership and continue to expand by suppressing Truth. There is no question that the failure to practice Christian ethics or divine standards has contributed to setting one religion against another, resulting in a consuming conflict that destroys the noble efforts of both organizations.

No organization or person can be or express something that is not within his capacity. If you dye a white lamb black, beneath it all he is still a white lamb. People and religions, then, are no more than the fullness of their true spiritual and material realization.

A closed mind in religious matters convinces people that they have the only faith that leads to salvation. Such smugness caters to the human ego and closes the door to progress, preventing them from attaining a higher state of being.

Some organizations that in reality have little to give would seal their members within a proscribed dogma and bind them to their particular faith regardless of the effects upon the person. They would rather do this than free them and allow them to act upon their free will. The leaders of these faiths rule people by fear. They say other religions are false, that their founders are false prophets, their exponents deluded.

The Path of Mysticism Stands behind All True Religion

What, then, is the reality behind religion? It is mysticism, for religious mysticism is awareness of God. The mystical path is the all-embracing nature of God that covers every area of human life.

God is both simple and complex. He is harmony—yet the reason men do not express harmony is that they have misqualified it by their own thoughts and feelings without recognizing that they do so. But a day of reckoning is at hand, and the one Path above the many—the mystical path, which seeks expression in the many—is now appearing, even as it has always been in the world.

The Open-Minded Way of Truth

One of the grossest fallacies of human nature is the tendency to honor that which one can accept and to dishonor that which seems unacceptable. This causes people to seek their friends among those who agree with them and to shun what they conceive of as the opposition.

But much can be learned from one's opponents. First of all, there is always the chance that they may be right—and if not, they may partially realize some phase of reality exceeding one's own. There is great value, then, in keeping an open mind toward the one Path above the many and extricating oneself from the sense that one has chosen absolutely right.

A true religion must include progressive revelation, or it is already stagnating. How limiting it is to steel oneself in personal righteousness and to adopt ideas that prevent seeing beyond one's own nose. Yet being tethered to some degree of spiritual reality—not dogma, but cardinal Truth—is necessary. That is why the one Path above the many partakes of the ever-expanding fount of living Truth that resides in the heart of the Real Self.

Many religious orders pledge to impart great wisdom to their followers, promising them liberty and happiness in a future salvation. Those who speak disparagingly of such religion call it a pie-in-the-sky idea. We feel that while religion can bring great blessing to man in the future, it is also beneficial in the here and now.

The seeker seldom realizes whether or not religious orders can deliver what they promise. Who, in reality, can rend the veil of the future? Although near-death experiences often reveal the validity of religious truths, the man in the street has never returned from the dead to verify the truths his religion proclaims.

Your Oneness with God, My Oneness with God

Here is the beauty of the Ascended Masters' presentation of Truth. The Ascended Masters proclaim an essential monotheism, the existence of but one God. But, by the Universal Christ, they reveal the Truth of that one God to be the essential divine reality of each individual, which all can realize to the fullest.

Reunion with this one supreme God can only be accomplished through the mediatorship of one's own Christ Self and the Universal Christ. For unless the Universal Christ is equated with oneself by acceptance in deed as well as in faith, there is no true mediatorship.

When an individual reaches a certain stage in his development, the human monad is no longer identified with the mortal self. Rather, it identifies with the Universal Christ and is in effect one with the beloved Son, the only begotten of the Father.

Thus, on the one Path above the many, all are made to know this Universal Christ and to receive the seamless garment that Christ wore, as their own priceless heritage. Walking with the Christ before they become the Christ, they enter deeply into his consciousness and merit the gift of his graces. Having attained to the stature of the Christ, men then walk with God. This walk with God has existed from the foundation of the world.

Omnipresent Salvation

Some Christian interpreters believe that before the birth of the Lord Jesus, salvation and eternal victory were impossible to man. They believe that only after Jesus' birth were all men who profess him able to be saved by him. (This type of thinking has even been carried over to the Christian calendar, for which Jesus is seen not only as the mediator between God and man, but as a type of mediator of the time sequence of all history—the years before his birth being designated as B.C. and the years after his birth as A.D.) But such narrow views of salvation are but one of many interpretations of the significance of Jesus' advent.

We understand that those who lived before him have lived again, and many of them are still living among us. We understand why Jesus said, "Before Abraham was, I AM."[1] For he knew the timeless reality of the Universal Christ. In the pure interest of Truth we honor the Christ, who is the Truth. We do not honor many of the commonly held concepts concerning salvation because they are incomplete, hence ineffectual.

For instance, many believe the theological concepts involving the fall of Adam and Eve—that all men had the sentence of death passed upon them with the fall of Adam. They also believe in the concept of vicarious atonement: that Jesus, by his death on the cross, paid the penalty of this sentence for all of us. If this were the case, then when Jesus spoke the words "It is finished"[2] and gave up the ghost, at that precise instant all of the "original sin" of Adam would have been wiped out, and from thence onward, men would have had the gift of eternal life originally held by Adam prior to the Fall.

The Truth is that Jesus' advent was not the first opportunity for salvation that God has given to man. The Universal Christ was available from the beginning and was "the Lamb slain from the foundation of the world."[3]

Enoch, the seventh from Adam—walking with God through the Christ consciousness—was able to attain such oneness with Christ and with God that he no longer was an ordinary mortal and he never tasted of death. He entered directly into the ascension through his reunion with the Christ, who was the arbiter of all things from the beginning.[4]

Elijah, ascending into heaven in a chariot of fire, passed through the ritual of the ascension and achieved his immortal freedom. He subsequently appeared on the mountaintop with Moses to Peter, James and John when Jesus was transfigured before them.[5] A number of others did not taste of death. Some of these instances were recorded and some remain unrecorded in the annals of men.

Those who passed from the screen of life and the pages of history to reembody again and again, came down through the cycles of time to the time of Jesus and thus entered into the Christian dispensation. Yet in every age—the age of Gautama Buddha, of Mohammed, of Zarathustra, of Confucius and of Lao Tzu—benign individuals have contributed much to the well-being of man and to the kingdom of God.

Devotees from many cultures and many spiritual paths have sought God. But the all-powerful realization of the one Path above the many is reunion with God, by that grace which is behind the attainment of victory for every man.

A Jeweled Expression of Divine Reality

Every lifestream has a jeweled expression of divine reality to reveal to the world when he is ready. To make oneself ready, then, is the vital factor in Truth and the business of living. Each individual has a portion of the whole that is his own special lot, for no two people are alike. Thus, this message of God and the Word of God must go forth to Jew and Gentile, to bond and free, to wise and ignorant, to all in whom the Spirit of life is active and to those whose hopes appear dead indeed.

The power of Truth is the only means of salvation to the planet. It is a message of hope. Little kernels and crumbs from the LORD's table fall into waiting hungry hearts through the outreach of the many religions. But often men and women are not satisfied with the ordinary or with the idea of public acceptance. These have as their criteria, "Is it true? And will it produce for me and for my fellowmen the fruit of striving?"

These will quickly see that the gift of God to the world is himself. Only by receiving this priceless gift of his own divine reality can he become master of himself and thus hopefully an Ascended Being, able to aid others and carry on into the infinite.

And what is the infinite? Is it not the great circle that contains the little point of light that is the finite? The lesser is contained by the greater—and more than that, the lesser is a focal point of the greater in the process of revealing itself.

The one Path above the many shows an individual who is steeped in error and shrouded in darkness how he can be brought to the light and be cut free from human discord. Then he can be elevated to the stature of candidate for the ascension and ultimately become an Ascended Being.

The way of the cross is the forerunner to the ascension, yet man has stressed the cross and not the crown of the ascension. The divine purpose must be fulfilled. The one Path above the many sees salvation and liberty now, Truth now and progressive revelation forever.

Man must use the violet transmuting flame and be weaned from habits of wrong thought and feeling. Christlike concepts and modes of thought must be reestablished in each one.

The Path of the Seeker Who Becomes the Sought

The one Path above the many is that which men seek in the many. But if they find it not, they must continue to seek it until they do find it. They must never lose sight of their search for a high standard of faith and purity. This can be found in the religions of the world, so long as the seeker does not confine himself to "the letter that killeth."[6]

If the high standard of living Truth be adhered to in the spirit, it provides the blessed assurance that God will lead each one individually on his homeward way by the power of the Holy Spirit.

This one Path is the path of the spiritual avant-garde. It is the path of the lonely ones, until they have passed through the sea of troubles into the higher initiations. It is the path of the seeker who becomes the sought. It is the path of victory over the long night of error. It is the dawn that breaketh unto the eternal day.

Folly and the delusions of error melt away in the sunlight of Truth. Truth shows the face of God behind all things and demands that all things be shaped in the divine image by a conscious effort of the will. "Go, and do thou likewise" becomes a fiat to all. "This is my beloved Son"[7] is spoken to all. Truth becomes the personal charge of God that all learn to accept in the justice of creation.

God's Strength Is Your Strength

How can it be that the Universal God, who has given his intelligence and the gift of his creative heart to man, would cause that gift to fail? His infinite wisdom framed the world, the star systems, the radiant outreach of the mind, and the marvelous tributaries of the nerves and arteries in the physical body. Why, then, would he work for naught?

He will not do so, for God has given the gift of a divinely ordained future to us all. In our union with that precious gift lies our strength. In our division and our diversity lies the false sense of personal salvation that lauds the efforts of the ego while denying the efforts of God.

Without realizing what he does, man leans on the frail

staff of mortal opinion. He seeks his confessors, the old and familiar, and he finds there a pseudocomfort that will one day pale into insignificance when he learns the Truth.

Sooner or later, he must return to the feet of the Masters and perceive that the brotherhood of angels and men is a divine chorus whose anthems, universal in character, will lead all to "the place where the Lord lay." For where I am, there shall ye be also,[8] holding my hand as you journey, pilgrims all, upon the one Path above the many.

Notes

Introduction

1. Rev. 10:9. All Bible quotes are from the King James Version.
2. Ralph Waldo Emerson, *Representative Men: Seven Lectures* (Philadelphia: David McKay, 1893), pp. 286–87.
3. Jer. 31:33–34.
4. 2 Kings 5:1–15.

Chapter 1 · The Great White Brotherhood

1. Mic. 4:4.
2. Goddess of Liberty, *Pearls of Wisdom,* vol. 11, no. 26, June 30, 1968.
3. Mary Baker Eddy, *Science and Health with Key to the Scriptures* (Boston: First Church of Christ, Scientist, 1971), pp. 518, 264–65, 513, 515.
4. Maha Chohan, *Pearls of Wisdom,* vol. 9, no. 28, July 10, 1966.
5. Ibid.
6. Heb. 12:29. Exod. 3:2, 14.

7. Gautama Buddha, December 31, 1969.

8. Chananda with the Ascended Master Alexander Gaylord, "The Great White Brotherhood as Inner World Government," *Keepers of the Flame Lessons,* no. 5, pp. 15–20.

9. Goddess of Liberty, op. cit.

10. Great Divine Director, *Pearls of Wisdom,* vol. 9, no. 41, October 9, 1966.

11. Matt. 7:20.

12. Saint Germain, "From the Heart of Saint Germain," *Keepers of the Flame Lessons,* no. 12.

13. Quoted by the Maha Chohan, op. cit.

14. Goddess of Liberty, op. cit.

15. 1 John 4:1.

16. See Godfré Ray King, *Unveiled Mysteries* (Chicago: Saint Germain Press, 1939) and *The Magic Presence* (Chicago: Saint Germain Press, 1935).

17. El Morya, letter to "Beloved Hearts of Light," March 13, 1964.

18. El Morya, *The Chela and the Path* (Corwin Springs, Mont.: Summit University Press, 1976), chap. 7. For additional teaching and subsequent dispensations for mankind to visit the etheric retreats of the Brotherhood, see Gautama Buddha and Saint Germain, *Pearls of Wisdom,* vol. 29, no. 21, May 25, 1986. For an extensive description of the Seven Mighty Elohim and their retreats, see the bound volume of the 1978 *Pearls of Wisdom,* pp. 319–445.

19. Great Divine Director, October 9, 1966.

20. Acts 4:12. Great Divine Director, *Pearls of Wisdom,* vol. 9, no. 40, October 2, 1966.

21. Matt. 24:24; Mark 13:22.

22. 2 Cor. 11:14.

23. Great Divine Director, October 2, 1966.

24. El Morya, *Pearls of Wisdom,* vol. 11, no. 1, January 7, 1968.

Chapter 2 · Ascended and Unascended Masters

1. 2 Pet. 2:19.
2. Matt. 12:37.
3. Saint Germain, "Intermediate Cosmo-Science, Part II," *Keepers of the Flame Lessons,* no. 14.
4. Matt. 11:30.
5. Lady Master Venus, February 4, 1962.
6. Goddess of Purity, November 4, 1966.
7. Luke 1:17.
8. Matt. 14:1–12; 17:1–13.
9. Matt. 11:11.
10. 2 Kings 4–8.
11. John 3:30.
12. Matt. 3:3.
13. Matt. 3:3; 11:9–10. "A Letter from Beloved Chananda," *Keepers of the Flame Lessons,* no. 21.
14. This occurred on January 1, 1956.
15. Saint Germain, "Intermediate Cosmo-Science, Part I," *Keepers of the Flame Lessons,* no. 13.
16. Jer. 31:33–34.
17. Isa. 30:20–21.
18. James 3:17. Titus 1:15.
19. John 14:12.

Chapter 3 · The Summit Lighthouse

1. John 1:5.
2. Mark L. Prophet and Elizabeth Clare Prophet, *Lords of the Seven Rays* (Corwin Springs, Mont.: Summit University Press, 1986).

3. El Morya, letter to "Chelas Mine," August 8, 1958.

4. Zech. 4:6.

5. *New Encyclopaedia Britannica,* 15th ed., micropaedia, s.v. "Robinson, John." Willison, George F., *Saints and Strangers* (New York: Time-Life Books, 1945), p. 127.

6. Acts 1:11.

7. Matt. 7:14.

8. Matt. 5:14.

9. Mark 4:39.

10. Queen of Light, July 3, 1969.

11. Exod. 3:14.

12. John 1:1–3. John 14:6. John 11:25.

13. El Morya, *Pearls of Wisdom,* vol. 3, no. 34, August 19, 1960.

14. El Morya, *Pearls of Wisdom,* vol. 3, no. 36, September 2, 1960.

15. Lanto, *Pearls of Wisdom,* vol. 4, no. 20, May 19, 1961.

16. El Morya, letter to "My Beloved Friends of Light and Love," November 10, 1959.

17. El Morya, *Pearls of Wisdom,* vol. 4, no. 41, October 13, 1961.

18. El Morya, *Pearls of Wisdom,* vol. 4, no. 32, August 11, 1961.

19. Lanto, *Pearls of Wisdom,* vol. 10, no. 40, October 1, 1967.

Chapter 4 · The Messengers

1. Lord Lanto, *Pearls of Wisdom,* vol. 10, no. 39, September 24, 1967. Henry Wadsworth Longfellow, "A Psalm of Life."

2. Deut. 4:2. See also Rev. 22:18–19.

3. Heb. 13:8.

4. Rev. 22:10.

5. Kuthumi, *Pearls of Wisdom,* vol. 11, no. 44, November 3, 1968.

6. Isa. 30:20–21.

7. 1 Kings 4:25.

8. El Morya, *Pearls of Wisdom*, vol. 3, no. 35, August 26, 1960.

9. Saint Germain, *Pearls of Wisdom*, vol. 3, no. 10, March 4, 1960.

10. Maha Chohan, July 2, 1962.

11. Saint Germain, *Pearls of Wisdom*, vol. 10, no. 38, September 17, 1967.

12. Rom. 10:15.

13. John 4:10–14.

14. Casimir Poseidon, September 12, 1965.

15. Great Divine Director, July 5, 1970.

16. Rev. 1:1.

17. Isa. 53:3.

18. Rev. 11:3–13, 15–19.

Chapter 5 · The Divine Will

1. Luke 12:32.

2. El Morya, *The Sacred Adventure* (Corwin Springs, Mont.: Summit University Press, 1981), pp. 37–38.

3. Luke 22:42.

4. El Morya, op. cit., p. 82.

5. God Meru, November 27, 1966.

6. Archangel Michael, February 14, 1963.

7. Saint Germain, *Pearls of Wisdom*, vol. 4, no. 21, May 26, 1961.

8. Heb. 11:1. El Morya, op. cit., pp. 11–12.

9. El Morya, op. cit., pp. 57–58.

10. Himalaya, *Pearls of Wisdom*, vol. 3, no. 38, September 16, 1960.

11. Luke 22:44.

12. Luke 22:42.

13. John 14:15.

14. El Morya, op. cit., p. 105.

15. Suggested supplementary reading: *The Imitation of Christ,* by Thomas à Kempis.

16. Serapis Bey, "The Eternal Brotherhood," *Keepers of the Flame Lessons,* no. 13.

17. El Morya, op. cit., pp. 58–59.

18. 1 Cor. 15:50.

19. El Morya, op. cit., pp. 107–109.

20. Ezek. 18:20.

21. Exod. 20:3. El Morya, op. cit., pp. 25–26.

22. 1 John 1:5. Heb. 13:8.

23. Luke 6:31.

24. 1 John 4:18.

25. Prov. 3:11–12; Heb. 12:5–6.

26. Gal. 6:7.

27. Matt. 6:28. El Morya, op. cit., pp. 21–25.

28. Luke 23:34. Ps. 23:1–3.

29. Serapis Bey, *Dossier on the Ascension* (Corwin Springs, Mont.: Summit University Press, 1978), pp. 71–73.

30. Luke 17:33.

31. 2 Cor. 3:17.

32. Col. 3:3.

33. El Morya, op. cit., pp. 27–28.

34. Luke 9:62.

35. Kuthumi, *Pearls of Wisdom,* vol. 11, no. 22, June 2, 1968.

36. Matt. 16:23; Mark 8:33; Luke 4:8.

37. Matt. 24:24.

38. Matt. 24:26–27.

39. Rev. 22:11.

40. Kahlil Gibran, *The Prophet* (1923; reprint, New York: Alfred A. Knopf, 1973), p. 96.

41. Matt. 18:14; John 10:10.

42. El Morya, op. cit., pp. 28–30.

43. John 14:1; Matt. 19:26.

44. 2 Cor. 3:6.

45. John 14:16–17; 15:26; 16:13; 1 John 4:6.

46. El Morya, op. cit., pp. 89–91, 94–97.

47. Luke 15:11–32.

48. 1 Cor. 3:13. El Morya, op. cit., 67–68.

49. El Morya, op. cit., p. 42.

Chapter 6 · Planes of Consciousness

1. For a chart of the seven rays, the seven chakras and the beings who ensoul them, see the first book in this series: Mark L. Prophet and Elizabeth Clare Prophet, *Climb the Highest Mountain: The Path of the Higher Self* (Corwin Springs, Mont.: Summit University Press, 1986), pp. 564–65.

2. The spiritual sun behind the physical sun in the center of the universe is not positioned spatially behind the physical sun. It is congruent with or superimposed upon it in another dimension.

3. This perpendicularity cannot be adequately represented in three dimensions, let alone two.

4. The term "Matter," when referring to the planes of God's consciousness, does not imply the density "of the earth earthy" but a level or frequency that manifests as the coordinate of Spirit in the white fire core and in the purple-and-gold, violet, and pink spheres of the Great Central Sun.

5. Serapis Bey, December 29, 1978.

6. Elizabeth Clare Prophet, *Nurturing Your Baby's Soul: A Spiritual Guide for Expectant Parents* (Corwin Springs, Mont.: Summit University Press, 1998), pp. 100–102.

7. Mother Mary, *Pearls of Wisdom*, vol. 33, no. 41, October 21, 1990.

8. Ibid.

9. Saint Germain, *Pearls of Wisdom,* vol. 32, no. 55, November 11, 1989.

10. John 10:30. John 5:17.

11. Prov. 23:7.

12. Matt. 5:8.

13. C. W. Leadbeater, *The Chakras* (Wheaton, Ill.: Theosophical Publishing House, 1927), p. 32.

14. Ps. 121:8.

15. Gen. 28:12.

16. Matt. 17:1–8.

17. Matt. 28:18.

18. This refers to the rising seed atom or to the white-fire ball as it is visualized in meditation.

19. Amaryllis, December 6, 1970.

20. Mother Mary, September 19, 1976.

21. The Ascended Masters Kuthumi and Djwal Kul give exercises, meditations and visualizations for strengthening the aura and increasing the light in the chakras. They give practical tools for the spiritual seeker who wishes to work with the Law of his being as explained in this chapter. See Kuthumi and Djwal Kul, *The Human Aura* (Corwin Springs, Mont.: Summit University Press, 1996).

22. 2 Kings 2:11.

23. Mother Mary, *Pearls of Wisdom,* vol. 11, no. 39, September 29, 1968.

24. Gal. 6:7.

25. Matt. 6:23.

26. Goddess of Purity, September 13, 1970.

Chapter 7 · The One Path above the Many: Mysticism

1. John 8:58.
2. John 19:30.
3. Rev. 13:8.
4. Gen. 4:17; 5:22–24; Jude 14.
5. 2 Kings 2:11; Matt. 17:1–9.
6. 2 Cor. 3:6.
7. Luke 10:37. Matt. 3:17; 17:5.
8. Matt. 28:6. John 14:3.

Decree to Beloved Mighty Astrea

In the name of the beloved mighty victorious Presence of God, I AM in me, mighty I AM Presence and Holy Christ Selves of Keepers of the Flame, lightbearers of the world and all who are to ascend in this life, by and through the magnetic power of the sacred fire vested in the threefold flame burning within my heart, I call to beloved mighty Astrea and Purity, Archangel Gabriel and Hope, beloved Serapis Bey and the seraphim and cherubim of God, beloved Lanello, the entire Spirit of the Great White Brotherhood and the World Mother, elemental life—fire, air, water, and earth! to lock your cosmic circles and swords of blue flame in, through and around my four lower bodies, my electronic belt, my heart chakra and all of my chakras, my entire consciousness, being, and world.

[You may include here prayers for specific circumstances or conditions for which you are requesting assistance.]

Cut me loose and set me free [3x] from all that is less than God's perfection and my own divine plan fulfilled.

1. O beloved Astrea, may God Purity
   Manifest here for all to see,
   God's divine will shining through
   Circle and sword of brightest blue.

First chorus: Come now answer this my call
   Lock thy circle round us all.
   Circle and sword of brightest blue,
   Blaze now, raise now, shine right through!

2. Cutting life free from patterns unwise,
   Burdens fall off while souls arise
   Into thine arms of infinite love,
   Merciful shining from heaven above. [chorus]

3. Circle and sword of Astrea now shine,
   Blazing blue-white my being refine,
   Stripping away all doubt and fear,
   Faith and goodwill patterns appear. [chorus]

Second chorus: Come now answer this my call,
Lock thy circle round us all.
Circle and sword of brightest blue,
Raise our youth now, blaze right through!

Third chorus: Come now answer this my call,
Lock thy circle round us all.
Circle and sword of brightest blue,
Raise mankind now, shine right through!

And in full faith I consciously accept this manifest, manifest, manifest! [3x] right here and now with full power, eternally sustained, all-powerfully active, ever expanding, and world enfolding until all are wholly ascended in the light and free! Beloved I AM! Beloved I AM! Beloved I AM!

[Give each verse, followed by the first chorus; repeat the verses, using the second chorus; then give the verses a third time, using the third chorus.]

Glossary

Terms set in italics are defined elsewhere in the glossary.

Akashic records. All that transpires in an individual's world is recorded in a substance and dimension known as akasha (Sanskrit, from the root *kāś* 'to be visible, appear,' 'to shine brightly,' 'to see clearly'). Akasha is primary substance, the subtlest, ethereal essence that fills the whole of space—"etheric" energy vibrating at a certain frequency so as to absorb or record all of the impressions of life. These records can be read by adepts or those whose soul (psychic) faculties are developed.

Alpha and Omega. The divine wholeness of the Father/*Mother* God affirmed as "the beginning and the ending" by the Lord Christ in Revelation. Ascended *twin flames* of the *Cosmic Christ* consciousness, who hold the balance of the masculine/feminine polarity of the Godhead in the *Great Central Sun* of cosmos. Thus through the *Universal Christ,* the Word incarnate, the Father is the origin and the Mother is the fulfillment of the cycles of God's consciousness expressed throughout the *Spirit/Matter* creation. *See also* Mother. (Rev. 1:8, 11; 21:6; 22:13)

Ancient of Days. *See* Sanat Kumara.

Antahkarana. (Skt. for 'internal sense organ.') The web of life. The net of light spanning *Spirit* and *Matter,* connecting and sensitizing the whole of creation within itself and to the heart of God.

Ascended Master. One who, through Christ and the putting on of that Mind which was in Christ Jesus, has mastered time and space and in the process gained the mastery of the self in the *four lower bodies* and the four quadrants of *Matter,* in the chakras and the balanced *threefold flame.* An Ascended Master has also transmuted at least 51 percent of his karma, fulfilled his divine plan and taken the initiations of the ruby ray unto the ritual of the *ascension*—acceleration by the *sacred fire* into the Presence of the I AM THAT I AM (the *I AM Presence*). Ascended Masters inhabit the planes of *Spirit*—the kingdom of God (God's consciousness)—and may teach unascended souls in an *etheric temple* or in the cities on the *etheric plane* (the kingdom of heaven).

Ascension. The ritual whereby the soul reunites with the *Spirit* of the living God, the *I AM Presence.* The ascension is the culmination of the soul's God-victorious sojourn in time and space. It is the reward of the righteous that is the gift of God after the last judgment before the great white throne, in which each man is judged according to his works.

The ascension was experienced by Enoch, of whom it is written that he "walked with God; and he was not, for God took him"; by Elijah, who went up by a whirlwind into heaven; and by Jesus. Scripture records that Jesus was taken up by a cloud into heaven. This is commonly referred to as Jesus' ascension. However, the *Ascended Master* El Morya has revealed that Jesus lived many years after this event and made his ascension after his passing in Kashmir at the age of 81.

The reunion with God in the ascension, signifying the end of the rounds of karma and rebirth and the return to the LORD's glory, is the goal of life for the sons and daughters of God. Jesus said, "No man hath ascended up to heaven but he that came down from heaven, even the Son of man."

By her salvation ("Self-elevation"), the conscious raising up of the Son of God within her temple, the soul puts on her wedding garment to fulfill the office of the Son (sun, or light) of manifestation. Following the initiatic path of Jesus, the soul is made worthy by his grace to be the bearer of his cross and his crown. She ascends through the *Christ Self* to her LORD, the I AM Presence, whence she descended. (Rev. 20:12–13; Gen. 5:24; 2 Kings 2:11; Luke 24:50–51; Acts 1:9–11; John 3:13)

Causal Body. The body of First Cause; seven concentric spheres of light and consciousness surrounding the *I AM Presence* in the planes of *Spirit*, whose momentums, added to by the Good—the LORD's Word and Works manifested by the soul in all past lives— are accessible today, moment by moment as we need them.

One's spiritual resources and creativity—talents, graces, gifts and genius, garnered through exemplary service on the *seven rays*—may be drawn forth from the Causal Body through invocation made to the I AM Presence in the name of the *Christ Self.*

The Causal Body is the storehouse of every good and perfect thing that is a part of our true identity. In addition, the great spheres of the Causal Body are the dwelling place of the Most High God to which Jesus referred when he said, "In my Father's house are many mansions.... I go to prepare a place for you.... I will come again and receive you unto myself; that where I AM [where I, the incarnate Christ, AM in the I AM Presence], there ye may be also."

The Causal Body is the mansion, or habitation, of the Spirit of the I AM THAT I AM to which the soul returns through Christ Jesus and the individual Christ Self in the ritual of the *ascension.* The apostle Paul was referring to the Causal Body as the star of each man's individualization of the God Flame when he said, "One star differeth from another star in glory." *See also* Chart of Your Divine Self; color illustration facing page 74. (Matt. 6:19–21; John 14:2–3; 1 Cor. 15:41)

Chart of Your Divine Self. (See illustration facing page 74.) There are
three figures represented in the chart, which we will refer to as
the upper figure, the middle figure and the lower figure. The upper
figure is the *I AM Presence,* the I AM THAT I AM, God individualized for each of his sons and daughters. The Divine Monad
consists of the I AM Presence surrounded by the spheres (rings of
color, of light) that comprise the *Causal Body.* This is the body of
First Cause, which contains man's "treasure laid up in heaven"—
perfect works, perfect thoughts and feelings, perfect words—energies that have ascended from the plane of action in time and space
as the result of man's correct exercise of free will and his correct
qualification of the stream of life that issues forth from the heart
of the Presence and descends to the level of the *Christ Self.*

    The middle figure in the chart is the mediator between God
and man, called the Christ Self, the Real Self, or the Christ consciousness. It has also been referred to as the Higher Mental
Body or Higher Consciousness. The Christ Self overshadows
the lower self, which consists of the soul evolving through the
four planes of *Matter* in the *four lower bodies* corresponding to
the planes of fire, air, water and earth; that is, the etheric body,
the mental body, the emotional body and the physical body.

    The three figures of the chart correspond to the Trinity of
Father (the upper figure), Son (the middle figure) and Holy
Spirit. The lower figure is intended to become the temple for the
Holy Spirit, which is indicated in the enfolding violet-flame
action of the sacred fire. The lower figure corresponds to you as
a disciple on the *Path.* Your soul is the nonpermanent aspect of
being that is made permanent through the ritual of the *ascension.* The ascension is the process whereby the soul, having balanced his karma and fulfilled his divine plan, merges first with
the Christ consciousness and then with the living Presence of the
I AM THAT I AM. Once the ascension has taken place, the
soul—the corruptible aspect of being—becomes the incorrupt-
ible one, a permanent atom in the body of God. The Chart of
Your Divine Self is therefore a diagram of yourself—past, present and future.

The lower figure represents mankind evolving in the planes of Matter. This is how you should visualize yourself standing in the violet flame, which you invoke in the name of the I AM Presence and in the name of your Christ Self in order to purify your four lower bodies in preparation for the ritual of the alchemical marriage—your soul's union with the Lamb as the bride of Christ.

The lower figure is surrounded by a tube of light, which is projected from the heart of the I AM Presence in answer to your call. It is a field of fiery protection sustained in *Spirit* and in Matter for the sealing of the individuality of the disciple. The *threefold flame* within the heart is the spark of life projected from the I AM Presence through the Christ Self and anchored in the etheric planes in the secret chamber of the heart for the purpose of the soul's evolution in Matter. Also called the Christ Flame, the threefold flame is the spark of man's divinity, his potential for Godhood.

The *crystal cord* is the stream of light that descends from the heart of the I AM Presence through the Christ Self, thence to the four lower bodies to sustain the soul's vehicles of expression in time and space. It is over this cord that the energy of the Presence flows, entering the being of man at the top of the head and providing the energy for the pulsation of the threefold flame and the physical heartbeat. When a round of the soul's incarnation in Matter-form is complete, the I AM Presence withdraws the crystal cord, the threefold flame returns to the level of the Christ and the energies of the four lower bodies return to their respective planes.

The dove of the Holy Spirit descending from the heart of the Father is shown just above the head of the Christ. When the individual man, as the lower figure, puts on and becomes the Christ consciousness as Jesus did, the descent of the Holy Spirit takes place and the words of the Father (the I AM Presence) are spoken, "This is my beloved Son in whom I AM well pleased." *See also* color illustration facing page 74. (Matt. 3:17)

Chela. (Hindi *celā* from Skt. *ceṭa* 'slave,' i.e., 'servant.') In India, a disciple of a religious teacher or guru. A term used generally to refer to a student of the *Ascended Masters* and their teachings. Specifically, a student of more than ordinary self-discipline and devotion initiated by an Ascended Master and serving the cause of the *Great White Brotherhood.*

Chohan. (Tibetan for 'lord' or 'master'; a chief.) Each of the *seven rays* has a chohan who focuses the Christ consciousness of the ray, which is indeed the Law of the ray governing its righteous use in man. Having ensouled and demonstrated this Law of the ray throughout numerous incarnations and having taken initiations both before and after the *ascension,* the candidate is appointed to the office of chohan by the Maha Chohan, the "Great Lord," who is himself the representative of the Holy Spirit on all the rays.

The names of the chohans of the rays (each one an *Ascended Master* representing one of the seven rays to earth's evolutions) and the locations of their physical/etheric focuses follow.

First ray: El Morya, Retreat of God's Will, Darjeeling, India.

Second ray: Lanto, Royal Teton Retreat, Grand Teton, Jackson Hole, Wyoming, U.S.A.

Third ray: Paul the Venetian, Château de Liberté, southern France, with a focus of the *threefold flame* at the Washington Monument, Washington, D.C., U.S.A.

Fourth ray: Serapis Bey, the Ascension Temple and *Retreat* at Luxor, Egypt.

Fifth ray: Hilarion (the apostle Paul), Temple of Truth, Crete.

Sixth ray: Nada, Arabian Retreat, Saudi Arabia.

Seventh ray: Saint Germain, Royal Teton Retreat, Grand Teton, Wyoming, U.S.A.; Cave of Symbols, Table Mountain, Wyoming, U.S.A. Saint Germain also works out of the Great

Divine Director's focuses—the Cave of Light in India and the Rakoczy Mansion in Transylvania, where Saint Germain presides as hierarch.

Christ Self. The individualized focus of "the only begotten of the Father, full of grace and truth." The *Universal Christ* individualized as the true identity of the soul; the Real Self of every man, woman and child to which the soul must rise. The Christ Self is the mediator between a man and his God. He is a man's own personal teacher, Master and prophet who officiates as high priest before the altar of the Holy of Holies *(I AM Presence)* of every man's temple made without hands.

The advent of the universal awareness of the Christ Self in God's people on earth is foretold by the prophets as the descent of THE LORD OUR RIGHTEOUSNESS, also called The Branch, in the universal age at hand. When one achieves the fullness of soul-identification with the Christ Self, he is called a Christed (anointed) one, and the Son of God is seen shining through the Son of man. *See also* Chart of Your Divine Self; color illustration facing page 74. (John 1:14; Isa. 11:1; Jer. 23:5–6; 33:15–16; Zech. 3:8; 6:12)

City Foursquare. The New Jerusalem; archetype of golden-age, etheric cities of light that exist even now on the *etheric plane* (in heaven) and are waiting to be lowered into physical manifestation (on earth). Saint John the Revelator saw the descent of the Holy City as the immaculate geometry of that which is to be and now is in the invisible realms of light: "And I John saw the holy city, new Jerusalem, coming down from God out of heaven. . . . " Thus in order that this vision and prophecy be fulfilled, Jesus taught us to pray with the authority of the spoken Word, "Thy kingdom come on earth as it is in heaven!"

Metaphysically speaking, the City Foursquare is the *mandala* of the four planes and the quadrants of the *Matter* universe; the four sides of the Great Pyramid of Christ's consciousness focused in the Matter spheres. The twelve gates are gates of

Christ's consciousness marking the lines and the degrees of the initiations he has prepared for his disciples. These gates are the open doors to the twelve qualities of the *Cosmic Christ* sustained by the twelve *solar hierarchies* (who are emanations of the *Universal Christ*) on behalf of all who are endued with the *Spirit's* all-consuming fiery love, all who would in grace "enter into his gates with thanksgiving and into his courts with praise."

Unascended souls may invoke the mandala of the City Foursquare for the fulfillment of the Christ consciousness—as Above, so below. The City Foursquare contains the blueprint of the solar (soul) identity of the 144,000 archetypes of the sons and daughters of God necessary to focus the divine wholeness of God's consciousness in a given dispensation. The light of the city is emitted from the *I AM Presence;* that of the Lamb (the Cosmic Christ), from the *Christ Self.* The jewels are the 144 focuses and frequencies of light anchored in the chakras of the Cosmic Christ. (Rev. 21:2, 9–27; Ps. 100:4)

Cosmic Being. (1) An *Ascended Master* who has attained cosmic consciousness and ensouls the light/energy/consciousness of many worlds and systems of worlds across the galaxies to the Sun behind the *Great Central Sun.* (2) A being of God who has never descended below the level of the Christ, never taken physical embodiment, made human karma or engaged in sin but has remained a part of the Cosmic Virgin and holds a cosmic balance for the return of souls from the vale (veil) of sorrows to the Immaculate Heart of the Blessed Mother.

Cosmic Christ. An office in *hierarchy,* currently held by Lord Maitreya, holding the focus of the *Universal Christ* on behalf of mankind.

Cosmic Clock. The science of charting the cycles of the soul's karma and initiations under the twelve *hierarchies of the sun.* Taught by Mother Mary to Mark and Elizabeth Prophet for sons and daughters of God returning to the *law of the One* and to their point of origin beyond the worlds of form and lesser causation.

Also, the diagram representing the cycles of karma under the twelve solar hierarchies. *See also* figure 9.

Cosmic Law. The law that governs mathematically, yet with the spontaneity of mercy's flame, all manifestation throughout the cosmos in the planes of *Spirit* and *Matter.*

Cosmic Secret Service. *See* K-17.

Crystal cord. The stream of God's light, life and consciousness that nourishes and sustains the soul and her *four lower bodies.* Also called the silver cord. *See also* Chart of Your Divine Self; color illustration facing page 74. (Eccles. 12:6)

Darjeeling Council. A council of the *Great White Brotherhood* consisting of *Ascended Masters* and unascended *chelas,* led by El Morya and headquartered in Darjeeling, India, at the Master's *etheric retreat.* Members include Mother Mary, Kuan Yin, Archangel Michael, the Great Divine Director, Serapis Bey, Kuthumi, Djwal Kul and numerous others, whose objective is to train souls for world service in God-government and the economy, through international relations and the establishment of the inner Christ as the foundation for religion, education and a return to golden-age culture in music and the arts.

Deathless solar body. *See* Seamless garment.

Decree. *n.* a foreordaining will, an edict or fiat, an authoritative decision, declaration, a law, ordinance or religious rule; a command or commandment. *v.* to decide, to declare, to determine or order; to ordain, to command or enjoin; to invoke the presence of God, his light/energy/consciousness, his power and protection, purity and perfection.

It is written in the Book of Job, "Thou shalt decree a thing, and it shall be established unto thee: and the light shall shine upon thy ways." The decree is the most powerful of all applications to the Godhead. It is the "Command ye me" of Isaiah 45:11, the original command to light that, as the "Lux fiat," is the birthright of the sons and daughters of God. It is the authoritative Word of God spoken in man by the name of the I *AM Presence* and the living Christ to bring about constructive change on earth through the will of God and his consciousness come on earth as it is in heaven—in manifestation here below as Above.

The dynamic decree offered as praise and petition to the LORD God in the science of the spoken Word is the "effectual fervent prayer of the righteous" that availeth much. It is the means whereby the supplicant identifies with the Word of God, even the original fiat of the Creator "Let there be light: and there was light."

Through the dynamic decree spoken with joy and love, faith and hope in God's covenants fulfilled, the supplicant receives the engrafting of the Word and experiences the transmutation by the *sacred fire* of the Holy Spirit, the "trial by fire" whereby all sin, disease and death are consumed, yet the righteous soul is preserved. The decree is the alchemist's tool and technique for personal and planetary transmutation and self-transcendence. The decree may be short or long and is usually marked by a formal preamble and a closing or acceptance. (Job 22:28; James 5:16; Gen. 1:3; James 1:21; 1 Cor. 3:13–15; 1 Pet. 1:7)

Dharma. (Skt. for 'law.') The realization of the Law of selfhood through adherence to *Cosmic Law,* including the laws of nature and a spiritual code of conduct such as the way or dharma of the Buddha or the Christ. One's duty to fulfill one's reason for being through the law of love and the sacred labor.

Dictations. The messages of the *Ascended Masters,* Archangels and other advanced spiritual beings delivered through the agency of the Holy Spirit by a *Messenger* of the *Great White Brotherhood.*

Discarnate entities. *See* Entities.

Divine Monad. *See* I AM Presence.

Electronic Presence. *See* I AM Presence.

Elementals. *See* Elohim.

Elohim. (Plural of Heb. *'Eloah,* 'God.') One of the Hebrew names of God, or of the gods; used in the Old Testament about 2,500 times, meaning "Mighty One" or "Strong One." Elohim is a uni-plural noun referring to the *twin flames* of the Godhead that comprise the "Divine Us." When speaking specifically of either the masculine or feminine half, the plural form is retained because of the understanding that one half of the Divine Whole contains and is the androgynous Self (the Divine Us).

The Seven Mighty Elohim and their feminine counterparts are the builders of form; hence, Elohim is the name of God used in the first verse of the Bible, "In the beginning God created the heaven and the earth." Serving directly under the Elohim are the four beings of the elements (the four cosmic forces) who have dominion over the elementals—gnomes (earth), salamanders (fire), sylphs (air) and undines (water).

The Seven Mighty Elohim are the "seven Spirits of God" named in Revelation and the "morning stars" that sang together in the beginning, as the LORD revealed them to his servant Job. There are also five Elohim who surround the white fire core of the *Great Central Sun.* In the order of *hierarchy,* the Elohim and *Cosmic Beings* carry the greatest concentration (the highest vibration) of light that we can comprehend in our state of evolution.

With the four beings of nature, their consorts and the elemental builders of form, they represent the power of our Father as the Creator (the blue ray). The Seven Archangels and their divine complements, the great seraphim, cherubim and all the angelic hosts represent the love of God in the fiery intensity of the Holy Ghost (the pink ray). The Seven Chohans of the Rays and all *Ascended Masters,* together with unascended sons and daughters of God, represent the wisdom of the Law of the Logos under the office of the Son (the yellow ray). These three kingdoms form a triad of manifestation, working in balance to step down the energies of the Trinity. The intonation of the sacred sound "Elohim" releases the tremendous power of their God Self-awareness stepped down for our blessed use through the *Cosmic Christ.*

Following are the names of the Seven Elohim, the rays they serve on and the locations of their *etheric retreats.*

First ray: Hercules and Amazonia, Half Dome, Sierra Nevada, Yosemite National Park, California, U.S.A.

Second ray: Apollo and Lumina, western lower Saxony, Germany.

Third ray: Heros and Amora, Lake Winnipeg, Canada.

Fourth ray: Purity and Astrea, near Gulf of Archangel, southeast arm of White Sea, Russia.

Fifth ray: Cyclopea and Virginia, Altai Range where China, Siberia and Mongolia meet, near Tabun Bogdo.

Sixth ray: Peace and Aloha, Hawaiian Islands.

Seventh ray, Arcturus and Victoria, near Luanda, Angola, Africa.

(Rev. 1:4; 3:1; 4:5; 5:6; Job 38:7)

Entities. Conglomerates of misqualified energy or disembodied individuals who have chosen to embody evil. Entities that are focuses of sinister forces may attack disembodied as well as embodied individuals. There are many different kinds of discarnate entities, including entities of liquor, marijuana, tobacco, death, sex and self-infatuation, sensuality, selfishness and self-love, suicide, anger, gossip, fear, insanity, depression, lust of money, gambling, weeping, various chemicals (including fluoride and sugar), horror, condemnation and sentimentality.

Etheric cities. *See* Etheric plane.

Etheric plane. The highest plane in the dimension of *Matter;* a plane that is as concrete and real as the physical plane (and more so) but is experienced through the senses of the soul in a dimension and a consciousness beyond physical awareness. The plane on which the *akashic records* of mankind's entire evolution register individually and collectively. It is the world of *Ascended Masters* and their *retreats,* etheric cities of light where souls of a higher order of evolution abide between embodiments. It is the plane of reality.

Here the golden age is in progress, love is the fullness of God's presence everywhere, and angels and elementals together with God's children serve in harmony to manifest Christ's kingdom in the universal age, worlds without end. As such it is the plane of transition between the earth/heaven realms and the kingdom of God, *Spirit,* or the Absolute. The lower etheric plane overlaps the astral/mental/physical belts. It is contaminated by these lower worlds occupied by the *false hierarchy* and the mass consciousness it controls, including its matrices and emotions.

Etheric retreats. *See* Etheric temples.

Etheric temples. Retreats of the *Ascended Masters* focused in the *etheric plane* or in the plane of the earth; anchoring points for cosmic energies and flames of God; places where the Ascended Masters train their *chelas* and to which the souls of mankind travel while out of their physical bodies.

False hierarchy. Beings who have rebelled against God and his Christ, including fallen angels, devils and the powers and principalities of Darkness who personify Evil (the Energy Veil). Those who deify and are the embodiment of Absolute Evil are referred to by the generic term "devil." Members of the false hierarchy referred to in scripture include Lucifer, Satan, the Antichrist, Serpent, and the accuser of the brethren.

Feminine ray. The light-emanation that comes forth from the *Mother* aspect of God.

Flaming Yod. A sun center, a focus of perfection, of God consciousness. The flaming Yod is the capacity of divinity within you to transform your being into an outpost of your Mighty *I AM Presence.*

Four lower bodies. The four lower bodies are four sheaths consisting of four distinct frequencies that surround the soul—the physical, emotional, mental and etheric, providing vehicles for the soul in her journey through time and space. The etheric sheath (highest in vibration) is the gateway to the three higher bodies: the *Christ*

Self, the *I AM Presence* and the *Causal Body. See also* Chart of
Your Divine Self; color illustration facing page 74.

Great Central Sun. Also called the Great Hub. The center of cosmos;
the point of integration of the *Spirit/Matter* cosmos; the point of
origin of all physical/spiritual creation; the nucleus or white fire
core of the cosmic egg. (Sirius, the God Star, is the focus of the
Great Central Sun in our sector of the galaxy.)

The Sun behind the sun is the spiritual Cause behind the
physical effect we see as our own physical sun and all other
stars and star systems, seen or unseen, including the Great Central Sun. The Sun behind the sun of cosmos is perceived as the
Cosmic Christ—the Word by whom the formless was endowed
with form and spiritual worlds were draped with physicality.

Likewise, the Sun behind the sun is the Son of God individualized in the *Christ Self,* shining in all his splendor behind the
soul and its interpenetrating sheaths of consciousness called the
four lower bodies. It is the Son of man—the "Sun" of every
*man*ifestation of God. The Sun behind the sun is referred to as
the "Sun of righteousness," which heals the mind, illumines the
soul and lights all her house. As "the glory of God," it is the light
of the *City Foursquare.* (Mal. 4:2; Rev. 21:23)

Great Hub. *See* Great Central Sun.

Great White Brotherhood. A spiritual order of Western saints and
Eastern adepts who have reunited with the *Spirit* of the living
God and who comprise the heavenly hosts. They have transcended the cycles of karma and rebirth and ascended (accelerated) into that higher reality which is the eternal abode of the
soul. The *Ascended Masters* of the Great White Brotherhood,
united for the highest purposes of the brotherhood of man under
the Fatherhood of God, have risen in every age from every culture and religion to inspire creative achievement in education,
the arts and sciences, God-government and the abundant life
through the economies of the nations.

The word "white" refers not to race but to the aura (halo)

of white light surrounding their forms. The Brotherhood also includes in its ranks certain unascended *chelas* of the Ascended Masters. Jesus Christ revealed this heavenly order of saints "robed in white" to his servant John in Revelation. *See also* Hierarchy. (Rev. 3:4–5; 6:9–11; 7:9, 13–14; 19:14)

Hierarchies of the sun. Cosmic Beings forming a ring of cosmic consciousness around the *Great Central Sun.* Each of the twelve hierarchies, one for each line of the *Cosmic Clock,* comprises millions of *Cosmic Beings* who ensoul the virtue of a line of the Clock. For example, the hierarchy of Capricorn focuses the virtue of God-power; the hierarchy of Aquarius focuses the virtue of God-love, and so on.

Each month you are given the torch and the flame of a hierarchy of the sun according to your cycles on the Cosmic Clock. You carry that flame through a set of initiations under that hierarchy. Thus for example, during the month that you are on the twelve o'clock line, you would be taking the initiations of God-power, and you would be tested in how well you can refrain from engaging in criticism, condemnation or judgment. *See also* figure 9.

Hierarchy. The universal chain of individualized God-free beings fulfilling the attributes and aspects of God's infinite Selfhood. Included in the cosmic hierarchical scheme are *Solar Logoi, Elohim,* Sons and Daughters of God, ascended and unascended Masters with their circles of *chelas, Cosmic Beings,* the twelve *hierarchies of the sun,* Archangels and angels of the sacred fire, children of the light, nature spirits (called *elementals*) and *twin flames* of the *Alpha/Omega* polarity sponsoring planetary and galactic systems.

This universal order of the Father's own Self-expression is the means whereby God in the *Great Central Sun* steps down the Presence and power of his universal being/consciousness in order that succeeding evolutions in time and space, from the least unto the greatest, might come to know the wonder of his love. The level of one's spiritual/physical attainment—measured by one's balanced self-awareness "hid with Christ in God" and demonstrating his Law, by his love, in the *Spirit/Matter* cosmos—is the criterion establishing one's placement on this ladder of life called hierarchy.

In the third century, Origen of Alexandria set forth his conception of a hierarchy of beings, ranging from angels to human beings to demons and beasts. This renowned scholar and theologian of the early Church, who set forth the chief cornerstone of Christ's doctrine and upon whose works subsequent Church Fathers, doctors and theologians built their traditions, taught that souls are assigned to their respective offices and duties based on previous actions and merits, and that each one has the opportunity to ascend or descend in rank.

Many beings of the heavenly hierarchy are named in the Book of Revelation. Apart from the *false hierarchy* of Antichrist, including the reprobate angels, some of the members of the *Great White Brotherhood* accounted for by Jesus are *Alpha and Omega,* the seven Spirits, the angels of the seven churches, the four and twenty elders, the four beasts, the saints robed in white, the two witnesses, the God of the Earth, the Woman clothed with the Sun and her Manchild, Archangel Michael and his angels, the Lamb and his wife, the 144,000 who have the Father's name written in their foreheads, the angel of the Everlasting Gospel, the seven angels (i.e., the Archangels of the *seven rays*) which stood before God, the angel clothed with a cloud and a rainbow upon his head, the seven thunders, The Faithful and True and his armies, and he that sat upon the great white throne. *See also* Elohim. (Rev. 1:4, 8, 11, 20; 2:1, 8, 12, 18; 3:1, 4–5, 7, 14; 4:2–10; 5:2, 6, 11; 6:9–11; 7:1–2, 9, 13–14; 8:2; 10:1, 3, 7; 11:3–4; 12:1, 5, 7; 14:1, 3–6, 14–19; 15:1; 16:1–4, 8, 10, 12, 17; 17:1; 18:1, 21; 19:4, 7, 11–17; 20:1; 21:6, 9; 22:13)

Human monad. The entire forcefield of self, the interconnecting spheres of influences—hereditary, environmental, karmic— which make up that self-awareness which identifies itself as human. The reference point of lesser awareness or nonawareness, out of which all mankind must evolve to the realization of the Real Self as the *Christ Self*.

I AM Presence. The I AM THAT I AM; the individualized Presence of God focused for each individual soul. The God-identity of the individual; the Divine Monad; the individual Source. The origin of the soul focused in the planes of *Spirit* just above the physical form; the personification of the God Flame for the individual. *See also* Chart of Your Divine Self; facing page 74. (Exod. 3:13–15)

K-17. Head of the Cosmic Secret Service. Referred to as "Friend," he takes on a physical body when assisting members of the various secret services of the nations of the world. His protective forcefield is a "ring-pass-not," a ring of white fire that may be tinged with the colors of the rays according to the requirement of the hour. He draws this circle of living flame around individuals and places to protect and to seal the identity and forcefield of those dedicated to the service of the light.

Both K-17 and his sister were able to sustain life in their physical bodies for over 300 years prior to their ascensions in the 1930s. Continuing their evolution and service to mankind, they now maintain a villa in Paris and focuses in other parts of the world for the training of unascended masters. K-17 and the legions in his command should be called upon to expose by the power of the All-Seeing Eye of God forces and plots that would undermine Saint Germain's plan for God-government in the golden age. K-17's flame is teal green and white.

Karmic Board. *See* Lords of Karma.

Keepers of the Flame Fraternity. An organization of *Ascended Masters* and their *chelas* who vow to keep the flame of life on earth and support the activities of the *Great White Brotherhood* in the establishment of their community and mystery school and in the dissemination of their teachings. Founded in 1961 by Saint Germain. Keepers of the Flame receive graded lessons in *Cosmic*

Law dictated by the Ascended Masters to their *Messengers* Mark and Elizabeth Prophet.

Lady Master Venus. *Twin flame* of Sanat Kumara. The focus of Lady Master Venus and her flame of beauty were anchored on the continent of Europe where the city of Vienna, Austria, stands today. It was through the ray anchored there that many of the Venusians embodied, bringing their culture with them. The German spelling of Vienna is "Wien," pronounced like the first three letters of "Venus." Not only the name, but also the culture, the art and the romantic feeling of this city of dreams are reminiscent of the planetary home of its founder. *See also* Sanat Kumara.

Laggards. *See* Maldek.

Law of the One. The property of God's wholeness that allows the body of God to be broken—as Jesus demonstrated at the Last Supper—yet still remain the One. In this manner, the Son of God can be personified in each child of God in the person of the Holy *Christ Self.* Through this light, every soul can accept the option to become the son of God, to unite with Christ and ascend back to God's heart, the heart of their own Mighty *I AM Presence.*

Lifestream. The stream of life that comes forth from the one Source, from the *I AM Presence* in the planes of *Spirit,* and descends to the planes of *Matter* where it manifests as the *threefold flame* anchored in the secret chamber of the heart for the sustainment of the soul in Matter and the nourishment of the *four lower bodies.* Used to denote souls evolving as individual "lifestreams" and hence synonymous with the term "individual." Denotes the ongoing nature of the individual through cycles of individualization.

Lifewave. *See* Manu.

Lodestone. The focus of the Father, of the masculine ray of the Godhead, which anchors the energies of *Spirit* in *Matter* at the crown chakra.

Logos. (Gk. for 'word,' 'speech,' 'reason'—the divine wisdom manifest in the creation.) According to ancient Greek philosophy, it is the controlling principle in the universe. The Book of John identifies the Word, or Logos, with Jesus Christ: "And the Word was made flesh and dwelt among us." Hence, Jesus Christ is seen as the embodiment of divine reason, the Word Incarnate.

Out of the word Logos, we derive the word logic, defined as "the science of the formal principles of reasoning." From logic comes geometry and the unfoldment and the articulation of the original Word of God as it is broken down into language and subject matter for the clear communication of knowledge. Thus, all knowledge is based on the original Word (with a capital W). Communicators of the original knowledge, which is the Logos, are communicators of the Word.

The Word also means Shakti, which is a Sanskrit term for 'energy,' 'power,' 'force.' Shakti is the dynamic, creative force of the universe—the feminine principle of the Godhead, who releases the potential of God from *Spirit* to *Matter.* Jesus Christ, the Word Incarnate, is also the Shakti of God. We see, then, that "to communicate the Word" is to communicate the original knowledge of God passed to man through his feminine aspect. It is also to communicate self-knowledge. In communicating this knowledge, we become conveyors of the Word and instruments of the Word.

Lords of Karma. The Ascended Beings who comprise the Karmic Board. Their names and the rays that they represent on the board are as follows: first ray, the Great Divine Director; second ray, the Goddess of Liberty; third ray, the Ascended Lady Master Nada; fourth ray, the Elohim Cyclopea; fifth ray, Pallas Athena, Goddess of Truth; sixth ray, Portia, the Goddess of Justice; seventh ray, Kuan Yin, Goddess of Mercy. Vajrasattva also sits on the Karmic Board.

The Lords of Karma dispense justice to this system of worlds, adjudicating karma, mercy and judgment on behalf of every *lifestream.* All souls must pass before the Karmic Board before and after each incarnation on earth, receiving their assignment and karmic allotment for each lifetime beforehand and the review of their performance at its conclusion.

Through the Keeper of the Scrolls and the recording angels, the Lords of Karma have access to the complete records of every lifestream's incarnations on earth. They determine who shall embody, as well as when and where. They assign souls to families and communities, measuring out the weights of karma that must be balanced as the "jot and tittle" of the Law. The Karmic Board, acting in consonance with the individual *I AM Presence* and *Christ Self,* determines when the soul has earned the right to be free from the wheel of karma and the round of rebirth. The Lords of Karma meet at the Royal Teton Retreat twice yearly, at winter and summer solstice, to review petitions from unascended mankind and to grant dispensations for their assistance.

Macrocosm. (Gk. for 'great world.') The larger cosmos; the entire warp and woof of creation, which we call the cosmic egg. Also used to contrast man as the *microcosm,* 'the little world,' against the backdrop of the larger world in which he lives.

Maldek. Once a planet in our solar system. The dark forces destroyed Maldek through the same tactics that today's manipulators use on earth to degrade the consciousness of the people. Its lifewaves waged a war ending in nuclear annihilation; the asteroid belt between Mars and Jupiter is what remains of the planet. The laggards are souls who came to earth from Maldek.

Mandala. (Skt. for 'circle,' 'sphere.') A group, company or assembly; a circle of friends; an assembly or gathering of Buddhas and Bodhisattvas. Also a circular design containing images of deities symbolizing the universe, totality, or wholeness; used in meditation by Hindus and Buddhists.

Manu. (Skt.) The progenitor and lawgiver of the evolutions of God on earth. The Manu and his divine complement are ascended *twin flames* assigned by the Father/Mother God to sponsor and ensoul the Christic image for a certain evolution or lifewave known as a root race—souls who embody as a group and have a unique archetypal pattern, divine plan and mission to fulfill on earth.

According to esoteric tradition, there are seven primary aggregations of souls—that is, the first to the seventh root races. The first three root races lived in purity and innocence upon earth in three golden ages before the fall of Adam and Eve. Through obedience to *Cosmic Law* and total identification with the Real Self, these three root races won their immortal freedom and ascended from earth.

It was during the time of the fourth root race, on the continent of Lemuria, that the allegorical Fall took place under the influence of the fallen angels known as Serpents (because they used the serpentine spinal energies to beguile the soul, or female principle in mankind, as a means to their end of lowering the masculine potential, thereby emasculating the Sons of God).

The fourth, fifth and sixth root races (the latter soul group not having entirely descended into physical incarnation) remain in embodiment on earth today. Lord Himalaya and his Beloved are the Manus for the fourth root race, Vaivasvata Manu and his consort are the Manus for the fifth root race and the God and Goddess Meru are the Manus for the sixth root race. The seventh root race is destined to incarnate on the continent of South America in the Aquarian age under their Manus, the Great Divine Director and his divine complement.

The Manus are beloved God-parents who respond instantaneously to the call of their children. The comforting presence of their light is endued with such great power/wisdom/love as to quiver the ethers and make each little one feel at home in the arms of God even in the darkest hour.

Masculine ray. The light-emanation that comes forth from the Father aspect of God.

Matter. The feminine (negative) polarity of the masculine (positive) *Spirit*. Matter acts as a chalice for the kingdom of God and is the abiding place of evolving souls who identify with their Lord, their Holy *Christ Self*. Matter is distinguished from matter (lowercase m)—the substance of the earth earthy, of the realms of maya, which blocks rather than radiates divine light and the Spirit of the I AM THAT I AM.

Messenger. Evangelist; one who goes before the angels bearing to the people of earth the good news of the gospel of Jesus Christ and, at the appointed time, the Everlasting Gospel. The Messengers of the *Great White Brotherhood* are anointed by the *hierarchy* as their apostles ("one sent on a mission"). They deliver through the *dictations* (prophecies) of the *Ascended Masters* the testimony and lost teachings of Jesus Christ in the power of the Holy Spirit to the seed of Christ, the lost sheep of the house of Israel, and to every nation. A Messenger is trained by an Ascended Master to receive by various methods the words, concepts, teachings and messages of the Great White Brotherhood. One who delivers the Law, the prophecies and the dispensations of God for a people and an age. (Rev. 14:6; Matt. 10:6; 15:24)

Microcosm. (Gk. for 'small world.') (1) The world of the individual, his *four lower bodies,* his aura and the forcefield of his karma. (2) The planet. *See also* Macrocosm.

Mother. The feminine polarity of the Godhead, the manifestation of God as Mother. Alternate terms: "Divine Mother," "Universal Mother" and "Cosmic Virgin." *Matter* is the feminine polarity of *Spirit,* and the term is used interchangeably with Mater (Lat. meaning 'mother'). In this context, the entire material cosmos becomes the womb of creation into which Spirit projects the energies of life. Matter, then, is the womb of the Cosmic Virgin, who, as the other half of the Divine Whole, also exists in Spirit as the spiritual polarity of God.

Jesus himself recognized *Alpha and Omega* as the highest representatives of the Father/Mother God and often referred to Alpha as Father and to Omega as Mother. Those who assume the feminine polarity of consciousness after the *ascension* are known as Ascended Lady Masters. Together with all feminine (femininely polarized) beings in the octaves of light, they focus the flame of the Divine Mother on behalf of the evolutions of mankind evolving in many systems of worlds. However, being androgynous, all of the heavenly host focus any of the masculine or feminine attributes of the Godhead at will, for they have entered the spheres of the divine wholeness.

Omega. *See* Alpha and Omega.

The Path. The strait gate and narrow way that leadeth unto life. The path of initiation whereby the disciple who pursues the Christ consciousness overcomes step-by-step the limitations of selfhood in time and space and attains reunion with reality through the ritual of the *ascension.* (Matt. 7:14)

Real Self. *See* Christ Self.

Reembodiment. Alternate term for reincarnation: the action of reincarnation; the state of being reincarnated. Rebirth in new bodies or forms of life, especially a rebirth of a soul in a new human body. The soul continues to return to the physical plane in a new body temple until it has balanced its karma, has attained self-mastery, has overcome the cycles of time and space and finally reunites with the *I AM Presence* through the ritual of the *ascension.*

Retreats. *See* Etheric temples.

Root race. *See* Manu.

Sacred fire. The Kundalini fire that lies as the coiled serpent in the base-of-the-spine chakra and rises through spiritual purity and self-mastery to the crown chakra, quickening the spiritual centers on the way. God, light, life, energy, the I AM THAT I AM. "Our God is a consuming fire." The sacred fire is the precipitation of the Holy Ghost for the baptism of souls, for purification, for alchemy and transmutation, and for the realization of the *ascension,* the sacred ritual whereby the soul returns to the One, the *I AM Presence.* (Heb. 12:29)

Sanat Kumara. The Ancient of Days, who volunteered to come to the earth thousands of years ago from his home on Venus. At that time, cosmic councils had decreed the dissolution of the earth, so great was mankind's departure from Cosmic Law. The Solar Lords had determined that no further opportunity should be granted humanity, who had willfully ignored and forgotten the God Flame within their hearts. The requirement of the Law for the saving of Terra was that one who qualified as the embodied Lamb be present in the physical octave to hold the balance and keep the *threefold flame* of life for and on behalf of every living soul. Sanat Kumara offered to be that one.

In his April 8, 1979, *Pearl of Wisdom,* Sanat Kumara told the story of how Venusian devotees volunteered to accompany him and embody among mankind to assist him to keep the flame: "The joy of opportunity was mingled with the sorrow that the sense of separation brings. I had chosen a voluntary exile upon a dark star. And though it was destined to be Freedom's Star, all knew it would be for me a long dark night of the soul.

"Then all at once from the valleys and the mountains there appeared a great gathering of my children. It was the souls of the hundred and forty and four thousand approaching our palace of light. They spiraled nearer and nearer as twelve companies singing the song of freedom, of love and of victory. . . . As we watched from the balcony, *Lady Master Venus* and I, we saw the thirteenth company robed in white. It was the royal priesthood of the Order of Melchizedek. . . .

"When all of their numbers had assembled, ring upon ring upon ring surrounding our home, and their hymn of praise and adoration to me was concluded, their spokesman stood before the balcony to address us on behalf of the great multitude. It was the soul of the one you know and love today as the Lord of the World, Gautama Buddha.

"And he addressed us, saying, 'O Ancient of Days, we have heard of the covenant that God hath made with thee this day and of thy commitment to keep the flame of life until some among earth's evolutions should be quickened and once again renew their vow to be bearers of the flame. O Ancient of Days, thou art to us our guru, our very life, our God. We will not leave thee comfortless. We will go with thee.'"

Thus they came to the earth with Sanat Kumara and legions of angels, preceded by another retinue of lightbearers who prepared the way and established the retreat of Shamballa—"City of White"—on an island in the Gobi Sea (now the Gobi Desert).

There Sanat Kumara anchored the focus of the threefold flame, establishing the initial thread of contact with all on earth by extending rays of light from his heart to their own. And there the volunteers from Venus embodied in dense veils of flesh to see the earth's evolutions through unto the victory of their vow.

The first from among these unascended lightbearers to respond to the call of Sanat Kumara from the physical octave was Gautama, and with him was Maitreya. Both pursued the path of the Bodhisattva unto Buddhahood, Gautama finishing the course first and Maitreya second. Thus the two became Sanat Kumara's foremost disciples, the first ultimately succeeding him in the office of Lord of the World, the second as *Cosmic Christ* and Planetary Buddha. *See also* Lady Master Venus.

Seamless garment. Light substance from the Son (sun) of God woven as the robe of consciousness worn by a Christed one. The Holy Spirit, as a great unifying coordinator, weaves the seamless garment from threads of God's light and love. The Maha Chohan teaches: "The shuttle of God's attention upon man drives forth radiant beams of descending light, scintillating fragments of purity and happiness toward earth and into the hearts of his children, whilst the tender risings of men's hopes, aspirations, invocations and calls for assistance do pursue the Deity in his mighty haven of cosmic purity."

Jesus likens weaving the seamless garment to preparing for a marriage: "To each man and each woman there is given the opportunity to prepare for the *ascension*. And none is deprived of the privilege of making himself ready. As a bride makes ready for her wedding day, filling the hope chest with the most precious linens and embroideries, so the soul makes ready for her reunion by garnering floral virtues, flame qualities that she appliqués upon the seamless garment. And none may participate in the marriage feast without a wedding garment."

Of this garment, Serapis Bey says: "When man functions under divine direction and activity either in or out of the body, he takes the energy dispensed to him that in ignorance might have been misused and creates instead a great body of light called the immaculate seamless garment of the living Christ, which will one day become the great spherical deathless solar body."

Seed atom. The focus of the Divine Mother (the feminine ray of the Godhead) that anchors the energies of *Spirit* in *Matter* at the base-of-the-spine chakra.

Seven rays. The light emanations of the Godhead. The seven rays of the white light that emerge through the prism of the Christ consciousness concentrating particular gifts, graces and principles of self-awareness in the *Logos* that can be developed through one's life calling. Each ray focuses a frequency or color, and specific qualities: (1) blue—faith, will, power, perfection and protection; (2) yellow—wisdom, understanding, enlightenment, intelligence and illumination; (3) pink—compassion, kindness, charity, love and beauty; (4) white—purity, discipline, order and joy; (5) green—truth, science, healing, music, abundance and vision; (6) purple and gold—ministration, service, peace and brotherhood; (7) violet—freedom, mercy, justice, transmutation and forgiveness.

The *Ascended Masters* teach that each of the seven rays of God is magnified one day of the week: Monday, the pink ray; Tuesday, the blue ray; Wednesday, the green ray; Thursday, the purple-and-gold ray; Friday, the white ray; Saturday, the violet ray; Sunday, the yellow ray.

The seven rays of the Elohim, the builders of form, are enshrined at the Royal Teton Retreat, an ancient focus of light congruent with the Grand Teton in Wyoming. The rays are concentrated and anchored in a large image of the All-Seeing Eye of God located in a council hall of the retreat.

Solar hierarchies. *See* Hierarchies of the sun.

Solar Logoi. *Cosmic Beings* who transmit the light emanations of the Godhead flowing from *Alpha and Omega* in the *Great Central Sun* to the planetary systems. In this capacity, they determine what quotient of light can be entrusted to the evolutions of earth.

Spirit. The masculine polarity of the Godhead; the coordinate of *Matter;* God as Father, who of necessity includes within the polarity of himself God as *Mother* and hence is known as the Father/Mother God. The plane of the *I AM Presence,* of perfection; the dwelling place of the *Ascended Masters* in the kingdom of God. (When lowercased, as in "spirits," the term is synonymous with discarnates, or astral *entities.* Singular and lowercased, "spirit" is used interchangeably with "soul.")

Threefold flame. The flame of the Christ that is the spark of life that burns within the secret chamber of the heart (a secondary chakra within the heart). The sacred trinity of power, wisdom and love that is the manifestation of the *sacred fire.*

Twin flame. The soul's masculine or feminine counterpart conceived out of the same white fire body, the fiery ovoid of the *I AM Presence.*

Universal Christ. The mediator between the planes of *Spirit* and the planes of *Matter.* Personified as the *Christ Self,* he is the mediator between the Spirit of God and the soul of man. The Universal Christ sustains the nexus of (the figure-eight flow of) consciousness through which the energies of the Father (Spirit) pass to his children for the crystallization (Christ-realization) of the God Flame by their souls' strivings in the cosmic womb (matrix) of the *Mother* (Matter).

The fusion of the energies of the positive and negative polarity of the Godhead in the creation takes place through the Universal Christ, the *Logos* without whom "was not any thing made that was made." The flow of light from the *Macrocosm* to the *microcosm,* from the Spirit (the *I AM Presence*) to the soul and back again over the figure-eight spiral, is fulfilled through this blessed mediator who is Christ the LORD, the true incarnation of the I AM THAT I AM.

The term "Christ" or "Christed one" also denotes an office in *hierarchy* held by those who have attained self-mastery on the *seven rays* and the seven chakras of the Holy Spirit. Christ-mastery includes the balancing of the *threefold flame*—the divine attributes of power, wisdom and love—for the harmonization of consciousness and the implementation of the mastery of the seven rays in the chakras and in the *four lower bodies* through the Mother Flame (raised Kundalini).

Expanding the consciousness of the Christ, the Christed one moves on to attain the realization of the Christ consciousness at a planetary level and is able to hold the balance of the Christ Flame on behalf of the evolutions of the planet. When this is achieved, he assists members of the heavenly hierarchy who serve under the office of the World Teachers and the planetary Christ. *See also* Chart of Your Divine Self; color illustration facing page 74. (John 1:1–14; 14:20, 23. Compare Rev. 3:8; Matt. 28:18; Rev. 1:18.)

Word. *See* Logos; Decree.

Yod. *See* Flaming Yod.

Spiritual Resources

If you would like to learn more
about other books, audiocassettes, CDs,
seminars and workshops featuring
the spiritual techniques discussed in this book,
please call 1-888-700-8087,
visit the Spiritual Transformation Network
at www.transformnet.org
or write Summit University Press, PO Box 5000,
Corwin Springs, MT 59030-5000 USA.
Fax 1-800-221-8307
(406-848-9555 outside the U.S.A.)

Other Titles from

SUMMIT UNIVERSITY ⚫ PRESS®

*Saint Germain's
Prophecy for the New Millennium*

The Lost Years of Jesus

The Lost Teachings of Jesus

*Climb the Highest Mountain:
The Path of the Higher Self*

Kabbalah: Key to Your Inner Power

*Reincarnation:
The Missing Link in Christianity*

Understanding Yourself

Messages from Heaven

Forbidden Mysteries of Enoch

Sacred Psychology of Love

The Human Aura

Saint Germain On Alchemy

The Path to Your Ascension

Quietly Comes the Buddha

POCKET GUIDES
TO PRACTICAL SPIRITUALITY:

How to Work with Angels

Creative Abundance

Soul Mates and Twin Flames

The Creative Power of Sound

Access the Power of Your Higher Self

Violet Flame to Heal Body, Mind and Soul

Summit University Press books are available at fine bookstores everywhere.

Mark L. Prophet and Elizabeth Clare Prophet are pioneers of modern spirituality. They are the authors of several best-selling books, such as *Saint Germain's Prophecy for the New Millennium*, *The Lost Years of Jesus*, *The Lost Teachings of Jesus*, *Saint Germain On Alchemy* and *Understanding Yourself*. Their books have been translated into fifteen languages.

The Prophets have also conducted seminars and workshops worldwide. Mark passed on in 1973 and Elizabeth has carried on their work.

Mrs. Prophet has been featured on NBC's "Ancient Prophecies" and has talked about her work on "Donahue," "Larry King Live!" "Nightline," "Sonya Live" and "CNN & Company."